AF600548

ARCHCONFRATERNITIES, ARCHSODALITIES AND PRIMARY UNIONS WITH A SUPPLEMENT ON THE ARCHCONFRATERNITY OF CHRISTIAN MOTHERS

This dissertation was approved by the Reverend Romaeus W. O'Brien, O.Carm., J.C.D., as director, and by the Reverend Meletius M. Wojnar, O.S.B.M., S.T.L., J.C.D., and the Reverend Frederick R. McManus, A.B., J.C.D., as readers.

THE CATHOLIC UNIVERSITY OF AMERICA
CANON LAW STUDIES
NO. 421

Archconfraternities, Archsodalities and Primary Unions With a Supplement on the Archconfraternity of Christian Mothers

A DISSERTATION

Submitted to the Faculty of the School of Canon Law of The Catholic University of America in Partial Fulfillment of the Requirements for the Degree of Doctor of Canon Law

BY
Rev. Edmund Quinn, O.F.M. Cap., B.A., J.C.L.
PRIEST OF THE PENNSYLVANIA PROVINCE OF SAINT AUGUSTINE

THE CATHOLIC UNIVERSITY OF AMERICA PRESS
WASHINGTON, D.C.
1962

Nihil Obstat:

MYLES SCHMITT, O.F.M. CAP., J.C.L.
Censor Deputatus

Washingtonii, die 17 maii, 1962.

Imprimi Potest:

GILES STAAB, O.F.M. CAP., S.T.D.
Minister Provincialis

Pittsburghi, die 18 maii, 1962.

Nihil Obstat:

ROMAEUS O'BRIEN, O. CARM., J.C.D.
Censor Deputatus

Washingtonii, die 30 maii, 1962.

Imprimatur:

✠PATRICIUS A. O'BOYLE, D.D.
Archiepiscopus Washingtoniensis

Washingtonii, die 5 iunii, 1962.

PRINTED BY
THE CAPUCHIN PRESS
PITTSBURGH, PENNSYLVANIA

TO
SAINT LAWRENCE OF BRINDISI
CAPUCHIN PRIEST
DOCTOR OF THE UNIVERSAL CHURCH

FOREWORD

Ecclesiastical societies have always enjoyed a place of importance in the life of the Church. In the course of time they have served the Church in spreading the faith, stimulating the practice of virtue by mutual aid and example among their membership, performing the spiritual and corporal works of mercy. They present a unified structure in whose framework laymen can readily exercise their apostolate. Particularly, in the 20th century, they offer a qualified instrument for Catholic Action and provide an organized effort whereby the teaching and activity of the Church can effectively influence the social and political orders.

In the historical development of ecclesiastical societies, the primary society made its appearance in the 16th century. This specific type of ecclesiastical association was created directly by the Holy See and given the power to affiliate other similar societies and communicate to them its Apostolic privileges and indulgences. The present study is concerned with three basic areas of interrelated investigation: the historical development of ecclesiastical associations up to the emergence of the primary society; the pre-Code common law, namely, the *Quaecumque* of Clement VIII (1592-1605), which served as the basic legislation for primary societies; and finally the present canonical norms dealing with primary societies.

May the writer express the hope that this study will be of legal aid to the moderators and officers of primary societies, and more particularly, that the supplement on the *Archconfraternity of Christian Mothers* will be of practical service to the many ecclesiastical associations of lay women. In view of the continued emphasis and expansion of the lay apostolate by the recent Roman Pontiffs, and "the progressive introduction of women into the modern apostolate,"[1] the pioneer efforts made by the many associations of Christian Mothers take on added importance and stand as a tribute to those who foresaw the effectiveness of these societies and encouraged their establishment.

[1]*Allocutio Pii XII ad Congressum Internationalem Apostolatus Laicorum*, 14 oct. 1951—*Acta Apostolicae Sedis, Commentarium Officiale* (Romae: Typis Polyglottis Vaticanis, 1909—), XLIII (1951), 785.

The writer wishes to take the occasion to thank his Capuchin Superiors for the opportunity of pursuing advanced studies in Canon Law, and to express his gratitude to the members of the Canon Law Faculty of Catholic University of America for their kind and gracious assistance. In particular, he wishes to thank the Reverend Romaeus O'Brien, O. Carm., who directed this dissertation. Finally, the writer expresses thanks to his confreres, Very Reverend Myles Schmitt, Fathers Harvey Dinkel, Vincent Rohr, and Finian Meis for their time and assistance, and very particularly, Sebastian Falcone who aided so greatly in the final revision of this work.

TABLE OF CONTENTS

PART ONE

HISTORICAL SYNOPSIS

PART TWO

CANONICAL COMMENTARY

Chapter V

Chapter VI

SUPPLEMENT

Chapter VII

PART ONE
HISTORICAL SYNOPSIS

INTRODUCTION

A general history of ecclesiastical associations of the faithful lies beyond the purpose of the historical section of this dissertation.[2] Such a cumbersome undertaking would entail a chronological analysis of the origin, organization and development of the individual associations, as well as an inquiry into the circumstances prevailing in the parishes and dioceses in which they have been established. A study of this type, even if circumscribed to a particular geographical area, would require painstaking consultation of the parish records and official archives of each ecclesiastical society to be treated. Moreover, a detailed history could do little more than chronicle the facts and factors underlying the beginnings of each association, furnish a chronologically arranged list of such societies, and perhaps focus some further attention on the causes and events which shaped their growth in time. Understandably, so pronounced a historical approach, for all of its other advantages, would contribute little, if anything, to a correct understanding of present canonical legislation.

Thus, the first section of this work furnishes only the historical highlights of the development of ecclesiastical associations which led to the creation of archconfraternities and primary unions. Due attention will be given to the general and particular legislation affecting primary societies prior to the Code of Canon Law. A careful analysis of the norms in question reveals at once the vitality and influence of these ecclesiastical associations in the various periods of Church history. Since the nature of every juridical entity is determined by its purpose and the means implementing that purpose, the ensuing historical chapters will consider, in particular, laws regulating the activities common to every primary association and underscore the elements essential to its juridical structure.

It is especially noteworthy that in the official designation and classification of ecclesiastical associations, neither the Holy See nor canonical authors have achieved standardization of terminology—a fact as true

2The terms *ecclesiastical association* and *ecclesiastical society* will be used interchangeably throughout this work.

today after the codification of Canon Law as it was before.[3] Mere designation of a particular society as a confraternity in its official title or statutes does not warrant the conclusion that it is on that account a true confraternity. It cannot be sufficiently stressed that the exact nature and juridical status of a particular association can only be inferred from a thorough and accurate analysis of the documents describing its institution, statutes, internal structure, common activity, customs and privileges. By reason of its antiquity such a society may not fit precisely into the various classifications contemplated by the Code of Canon Law; consequently, caution must guide the application of the laws in effect at the time of its founding.

It is hoped that this brief history will, on the one hand, afford valid and valuable insights into the rise and development of archconfraternities and primary unions, and, on the other hand, set in clear perspective the antecedents for the present canonical legislation. If this is accomplished, there will be established a valid standard for the study of particular primary societies.

[3]S. C. Ep. et Reg., *Romana,* 18 ian. 1907: "Porro vox confraternitatis in iure determinatum sensum non habet, quum etiam pro unione, congregatione, et pio opere usurpetur."—*Acta Sanctae Sedis* (41 vols., Romae: Ex Typographia Polyglotta, 1865-1908), XL (1907), 143 (hereafter cited: *ASS*). S. C. C., *Corrienten;* 13 nov. 1920: "Nota pariter divisio sumitur *confraternitatis* in *laicales* et *ecclesiasticas:* in qua divisione sumitur *confraternitas* pro qualibet societate seu associatione in finem pium inita."—*Acta Apostolicae Sedis, Commentarium Officiale* (Romae: Typis Polyglottis Vaticanis, 1909—), XIII (1921), 139 (hereafter cited: *AAS*).

CHAPTER I

BEGINNINGS AND EARLY DEVELOPMENT OF ECCLESIASTICAL ASSOCIATIONS

Article 1: The Early Centuries

The earliest Christian centuries witnessed a wide variety of associations of the faithful. In this respect the Church found parallels in the many religious, civic, and cultural associations which obtained among the Greeks and Romans. For this reason the early Church may well at times have appeared to her contemporaries as a federation of confraternities whose members, by their adherence to a simple statement of belief, were identified with a particular church having its own officers, specific policies, statutes, ceremonies and charitable works.[4] A more basic explanation, however, for the existence of societies in the early Church is rooted in the very psychology of man. The tendency to associate is a primary human expression, which assumes added significance under religious motivation: "Where two or three are gathered together for My sake, there I am in the midst of them."[5] Nor is the influence of workaday circumstances to be overlooked. Among the impelling motives which urged the early Christians to unite in associations were the collection of alms for the poorer churches,[6] and the administration and care of the common property.[7]

A fairly common phenomenon among the Christian laity at this early period was the organization of burial societies. Established to ensure a Christian burial, their exact juridical structure remains a matter for speculation in the absence of documents relating to their institution or definite approbation by the Church. Within the Roman Empire itself *collegia tenuiorum* were organized and awarded official status by civil

4Cf. Le Bras, G., "Les Confréries Chrétiennes: Problèmes et Propositions," *Revue Historique de Droit Français et Étranger,* XIX (1940-1941), pp. 311-312 (hereafter cited "Les Confréries," *RHDFE*).

5Mt 18, 20.

61 Cor. 16, 1.

7Acts 2, 44.

law.[8] In view of this fact, the Christian burial societies may possibly have achieved formal recognition by civil authority and may have existed in the Church not as ecclesiastical but as private societies.

However, there is no dearth of evidence that Constantine made provision for a group of *lectiarii,* whose members, by no means restricted to the clergy, assumed responsibility for the decent interment of the dead.[9] This group was expected to offer the service free of charge in behalf of the poor, although in some cases special endowments were established for this purpose.[10] The Fathers of the Church[11] make frequent references to these societies. Tertullian, in particular, speaks of a special trust fund maintained by Christian generosity for the burial of the poor.[12]

The Theodosian Code embodies references to the *parabalani,*[13] a group whose members served as hospital attendants. The tenor, if not the text of the law, assigns the *parabalani* a social status subordinate to the clergy in rank.[14] Their members were not to exceed a determined

[8]D (3.4) 1; D (47.22) 1.

[9]They are also referred to as *Copiatae.*—N (43.1). Cf. Rush, A., *Death and Burial in Christian Antiquity,* The Catholic University of America Studies in Christian Antiquity, n. 1 (Washington, D.C.: The Catholic University of America Press, 1941), pp. 111-112.

[10]N (43.1).

[11]St. Gregory of Nyssa, *De Vita S. Macrinae*—Migne, *Patrologiae Cursus Completus, Series Graeca* (161 vols., Parisiis, 1856-1866), XLVI, col. 985 (hereafter cited *MPG*); St. Jerome, *Epistola 1 (Ad Demetriadem Virginem),* 10—Migne, *Patrologiae Cursus Completus, Series Latina* (221 vols., Parisiis, 1844-1864), XXX, col. 27 (hereafter cited *MPL*); St. Augustine, *Confessiones,* IX, 12, 31—*MPL,* XXXII, cols. 776-777.

[12]Tertullian, *Apologeticum,* 39, 6—*Corpus Christianorum Series Latina* (Turnholti: Typographi Brepols, 1954), I, p. 151. Cf. Leclercq, H., "Fossoyeurs," *Dictionnaire D'Archéologie Chrétienne et de Liturgie,* eds. Cabrol and Leclercq (15 vols. in 30, Paris: Libraire Letouzey et Ané, 1923-1953) V[2] (1923), col. 2065 (hereafter cited *DACL*).

[13]C. Th. (16.2) 42 and 43; C (1.3) 17 and 18.

[14]The formulation of the law, dated September 29, 416, clearly classifies the *parabalani* and the clerics as two distinct states. After specific consideration of the clerical rank, Theodosian significantly adds: "praeterea eos qui parabalani vocantur." There is no cogent basis here for equating the *parabalani* with some type of minor order in the early Church. Cf. Leclercq. H., "Parabalani," *DACL,* XIII[2] (1938), col. 1577.

number. Candidates might be drawn only from the poorer class.[15] Apart from continuing discussion whether this group had ecclesiastical approbation in its own right or was established as a minor order in the early Church of Alexandria as the *fossores* were in Rome,[16] one fact remains unchallenged: the *parabalani* were dependent on the Bishop, and their work in behalf of the sick was under the supervision of Church authorities.[17]

At the beginning of the 4th century another group emerges—the *philopones* (spoudaei)[18] who, before long, spread all over the Near East.[19] Their purpose was to assist in the liturgical services, for the most part by the chanting of psalms and by participating in the various ecclesiastical processions. Both men and women were eligible for membership in the *philopones*. In Constantinople, under the guidance of St. John Chrysostom, they attained organizational standards which anticipate, and even elicit favorable comparison with, the organization of confraternities as set forth in the Code of Canon Law.[20] Of all the early Christian societies, the *philopones* were the closest to the concept of ecclesiastical association as contemplated in the Church's current legislation.[21] In the 4th and 5th centuries their exclusive religious pur-

[15] C. Th. (16.2) 42 and C (1.3) 18.

[16] Cf. H. Leclercq's extensive treatment in two separate entries in *DACL:* "Fossoyeurs," V2 (1923), cols. 2065-2092, and "Parabalani," XIII2 (1938), cols. 1574-1578. Cf. also Kurtscheid, B., *Historia Iuris Canonici, Historia Institutorum* (2. ed., Rome: Catholic Book Agency, 1951), p. 50 ff., where the *diaconissae* and *viduae* in the early Eastern and Western Churches are discussed. The frequent references to the *diaconissae* and their seemingly manifold duties might perhaps be better understood if the *diaconissae* (as well as the *viduae*) were regarded as members of an ecclesiastical association and not of an ecclesiastical state. As already indicated, the concept of an ecclesiastical association was by no means foreign to the early Church, completely surrounded as she was by private Roman and Greek societies, and in fact drawing her members from these same Roman and Greek elements.

[17] C (1.3) 17. Cf. Duhr, J., "La Confrérie dans la Vie d'Église," *Revue d'Histoire Ecclesiastique,* XXXV1 (1939), p. 445 (hereafter cited, "La Confrérie," *RHE*).

[18] These are first mentioned in a letter (ca. 312) of Bishop Peter the Martyr, Patriarch of Alexandria. Cf. Leclercq, H., "Confréries," *DACL,* III2 (1948), col. 2553.

[19] They are to be found in Constantinople, Jerusalem, Egypt, Beyrouth, Antioch and Pisidien. Concise historical notes on each association are given by Leclercq, H., "Confréries," *DACL,* III2 (1948), cols. 2554 ff.

[20] C. Th. (16.5) 7 and 11. *MPG,* LXVII, col. 1576.

[21] Duhr, J., "La Confrérie," *RHE,* XXXV1 (1939), p. 447. Consult also Lambert

pose, namely, participation in public worship, served as a guarantee of religious zeal and charity. Throughout this period they were, as a society, subject to the supervision and direction of ecclesiastical authority.[22]

Article 2: Monasticism and the Purgatorial Society

The chief factor in the development of ecclesiastical associations during the 8th and 9th centuries was the rapid expansion of Western Monasticism. In fact, the spiritual impact of monasticism on the laity in these centuries gave rise to a particular type of association, the purgatorial society.[23] Fundamental doctrines, such as the Communion of Saints, vicarious penance, the satisfactory value of meritorious acts, the efficacy of suffrages, furnished a dogmatic substratum for this particular ecclesiastical society. But it was the Benedictine monks who deserve credit for its far-reaching and influential development during this period.[24] Kings, nobles, knights, men and women, rich and poor enrolled in these monastically sponsored associations in order to share in the prayers and spiritual works of the monks. These devout persons beyond the cloister walls were motivated by the desire to ensure for themselves, while still alive, a perpetual memento in monastic prayers and penances.[25]

As early as the 8th century documentary materials show that various abbeys were exchanging reciprocal promises of prayers and spiritual works for the living and dead members of the monastic community.[26]

A., "Apotactites et Apotaxamenes," *DACL*, I2 (1924), cols. 2604-2626.

22Leclercq, H., "Parabalani," *DACL*, XIII2 (1938), col. 1577.

23Cf. Ebner, A., *Die kloesterlichen Gebets-verbruederungen* (Regensburg, 1890), p. 3.

24Le Bras, G., "Les Confréries," *RHDFE*, XIX (1940-1941), p. 314.

25A typical formulary of spiritual privileges accruing to enrolled members reads: "... in Mass and in Matins, in vigils and in prayers, in fastings and alms, and of all the good works which shall be done in this house forever..." Cf. the Consuetudinary of St. Augustine cited in "Some Ancient Benedictine Confraternity Books," *Downside Review*, IV (1885) p. 10. In this article Shepton Mallet considers 3 ancient confraternity books: one from St. Gallen which contains lists (dating back as early as 720) of members enrolled in the society; the Reichenau manuscript (which goes back to the year 826) and the Pfaffers confraternity book (dated 830).

26St. Boniface (680-754) wrote to the Abbot Optat of Mont Cassin, "... ut fami-

It was not long before members of the secular clergy gained admittance into these purgatorial associations,[27] and laymen were likewise accepted in great numbers, as the old confraternity books testify.[28]

In the second half of the 8th century the diocesan clergy, in imitation of their monastic counterpart, also instituted and propagated societies, enrollment in which guaranteed prayerful remembrance after death.[29] At the Council of Attigny (762), those present reciprocally committed themselves to a certain number of Masses and prayers in behalf of the assembled members after death.[30] Later councils repeated the same legislation, so that by the closing decades of the 9th century, an extensive network of purgatorial societies was operative through the Christian world.[31]

Article 3: Guilds and Ecclesiastical Societies

The mutual influence of the monastic association and the medieval guild is a matter of historical record, even if the specific degree of this interrelationship is difficult to assess. The medieval guilds, although not in the strict sense ecclesiastical societies, were characterized by well-defined religious activities, many of them directly related to the liturgical cycle. The statutes of many of these guilds prescribed works of

---

liaritatis fraternae caritatis inter nos sit et pro viventibus oratio communis et pro migrantibus de hoc saeculo orationes et missarum sollemnia celebrentur, cum alternatim nomina defunctorum inter nos mittantur."—*Monumenta Germaniae Historica, Epistolae Selectae, I, S. Bonifatii et Lulli Epistolae* (ed. Michael Tangl, Berolini, 1916), pp. 231-232.

27Cf. *Monumenta Germaniae Historica, Legum Sectio III, Concilia,* Tom. II, pars I (recensivit Albertus Werminghoff, Hannoverae et Lipsiae, 1904), p. 72: in the Council of Attigny (762) "... quando quislibet de hoc saeculo migraverit, centum psalteria et presbiteri ejus speciales missas centum cantent. Ipse autem Episcopus per se 30 missas impleat ... et presbiteri eorum centum missas et monachi centum psalteria psallere meminerunt." Cf. also the Council of Frankfort (794)—*MGH, ibid.,* p. 110.

28Cf. Mallet, S., "Some Ancient Benedictine Confraternity Books," *Downside Review,* IV (1885), pp. 2-14.

29Cf. *MGH, Epistolae Selectae, I, St. Bonifatii et Lulli Epistolae,* p. 157.

30*MGH, Legum Sectio III, Concilia,* Tom. II, pars I, p. 72.

31Cf. Council of Salzburg (799)—*MGH, Leges I, Capitularia Regum Francorum* (ed. Pertz, 1835), p. 81; Freising (805)—*MGH, Leges III, Leges Nationum Germanicarum* (ed. Pertz, Hannoverae, 1863), p. 479.

charity in behalf of the living and suffrages in behalf of the deceased members.[32] Because the guilds had their own patron saints, public meetings, and later on religious processions, it is difficult in certain instances to distinguish between an early guild and a genuine ecclesiastical association.[33]

All factors considered, it is safe to select the middle of the 9th century as the period in which the ecclesiastical society (as here discussed) finally came of age. Apart from any relationship with the guilds, the ecclesiastical association of the 9th and 10th centuries emerged as a type of organic body possessing internal government, dependent on episcopal vigilance, and, where serving religious or charitable purposes, at least tolerated in the parishes of the diocese. In 852, Hincmar of Rheims expressly banned societies whose meetings were characterized by excessive eating and drinking, quarreling and revelry. This enactment moreover carried a penalty of degradation against a cleric and expulsion for a layman who dared to contravene its provisions. The prelate insisted that the members of these societies should restrict themselves to mutual prayers and works of charity.[34]

[32]Lambert, J., *Two Thousand Years of Gild Life* (London: Hull, 1891), p. 6.

[33]Beringer, F.-Steinen, P., *Die Ablaesse, Ihr Wesen und Gebrauch* (2 vols., Paderborn: Ferdinand Schoeningh, 1921-1922), II, nn. 5-6 (hereafter cited *Die Ablaesse*).

[34]Mansi, *Sacrorum Conciliorum Nova et Amplissima Collectio* (53 vols. in 59, Parisiis-Arnhem-Leipzig, 1901-1927), XV, 479 (hereafter cited: Mansi). This text together with others was attributed to a Council of Nantes (Mansi, XVIII, 170) by Reginon de Prüm and dated as early as 658 by many authors and scholars. The reason for Reginon's forgery is uncertain but the fact that he fabricated the Council of Nantes has only recently become apparent, as earlier works on confraternities readily attest. Cf. Fournier, P.-Le Bras, G., *Histoire des Collections Canoniques en Occident* (2 vols., Paris: Recueil Sirey, 1931-1932), I, p. 259. On intrinsic consideration it seems certain that Hincmar's legislation refers to ecclesiastical associations and not to private societies or guilds. He makes reference only to religious functions and to works of a strictly religious nature: "in omni obsequio religionis coniunguntur: videlicet in oblatione, in luminaribus, in oblationibus mutuis, in exsequiis defunctorum, in eleemosynis, et caeteris pietatis officiis." Specific penalties are set forth for transgressors according to their vocational status, and, because women were admitted into ecclesiastical associations from the very beginning, it is not unusual to read: "...adeo penitus interdicimus, ut qui de cetero hoc agere praesumpserit, si presbyter fuerit, vel quilibet clericus, gradu privetur, si laicus, vel *femina,* usque ad satisfactionem separetur." Cf. Clarke, Thomas J., *Parish Societies,* The Catholic University of American Canon Law Studies, n. 176 (Washington, D.C.: The Catholic University of America Press, 1943), p. 14, who considers this legislation to be

By the 11th century there is ample evidence for the spread throughout Italy of ecclesiastical societies having marked organizational features. In Naples, Florence, and Venice, men and women assembled together under ecclesiastical direction to promote devotion to the saints, ensure spiritual assistance, provide for the needs of the poor, visit and nurse the sick, pray in common for dead members, and have Masses offered for them.[35] At the same time many associations lost sight of their original purpose and relaxed their vigilance against insidious abuses. Some associations began to stipulate that their members take an oath of mutual assistance against common enemies.[36] Frequent banqueting, excesses in eating and drinking at their meetings, scandalous quarrels, petty and prolonged bickerings among members elicited a wide range of synodal legislation.[37] Many bishops found it necessary to remind the faithful through their diocesan synods that ecclesiastical societies could only be established with the consent of the local Ordinary.[38] In Rome, before the middle of the 13th century, Pope Gregory IX (1227-1241) issued a decree to the effect that no ecclesiastical association could be established in the city without the special permission of the Holy See.[39]

Article 4: Mendicants and the Confraternities

The impact of the Mendicant Orders on the laity of the Middle Ages should not be gauged only in terms of the great numbers that embraced the religious life. A more significant criterion is found in the enthu-

---

concerned with guilds.

35Monti, G., *Le Confraternite Medievali dell'Alta et Media Italia* (2 vols., Venezia: "La Nuova Italia" editrice, 1927), I, pp. 70-73; Schnuerer, G., *Kirche und Kultur in Mittelalter* (3 vols., Paderborn: Ferdinand Schoeningh, 1927-1929), II, p. 453 ff.

36Contemporary legislation tellingly reveals a preoccupation with this abuse. *MGH, Leges I, Capitularia*, pp. 74, 135, 230, 352, 553. Cf. Council of Rouen (1189)—Mansi, XXII, 585; Montpillier (1214)—Mansi, XXII, 949; Toulouse (1229)—Mansi, XXIII, 203.

37Cf. councils mentioned in the foregoing footnotes and also the Synod Strigoniensis (Synod of Esztergom, Hungary, 1114)—Mansi, XXI, 108-109.

38Montpellier (1214)—Mansi, XXII, 949; Arles (1234)—Mansi, XXIII, 339. Cf. Duhr, J., "La Confrérie," *RHE*, XXXV (1939), pp. 468, 473.

39Gregory IX, const. *"Ad Nostrum,"* 26 oct. 1232—*Bullarum Diplomatum et Privilegionum Sanctorum Romanorum Pontificum Taurinensis Editio* (25 vols., Augustae Taurinensis, 1857-1872), III, p. 474 (hereafter cited *Bull. Rom. Taur.*).

siastic response of the various social classes to the Third Orders of St. Francis and St. Dominic.[40] The penitential spirit, poverty, and humility of the friars exerted a magnetic force upon the piety of the 13th century. As a result, countless numbers identified themselves with the Franciscan and Dominican spirit by adopting a religious rule of life specifically designed for the uncloistered masses. But the extensive influence of the mendicants struck even deeper roots. Under the guidance of the two orders, a new emphasis came to bear upon the formation and effectiveness of the ecclesiastical society, known as the confraternity. As the Benedictines of earlier times, the Franciscans and Dominicans united their benefactors into confraternities under the protection of the patron saints of their churches and convents.[41] In fact, many of the old confraternities dedicated to the Blessed Virgin Mary date back to this period.[42] The purpose of these confraternities was to foster devotion to the Blessed Virgin Mary and the saints by the arrangement of solemn prayer services and processions on major feast days. Special sermons were preached on these occasions, and special indulgences were granted to members in attendance. The regular confraternity meetings afforded an excellent opportunity to instruct the faithful in the fundamentals of the Catholic faith.[43] Among the particular works of charity

---

This constitution was directed primarily against a group of laymen who had organized a burial society in Rome without proper authorization.

[40]Cf. Reinmann, Gerald J., *The Third Order Secular of St. Francis,* The Catholic University of America Canon Law Studies, n. 50 (Washington, D.C.: The Catholic University of America, 1928), p. 21 ff.

[41]Cf. Meersseman, G., "Les Confréries de Sainte Dominique," *Archivum Fratrum Praedicatorum,* XX (1950), p. 18.

[42]*Bullarium Ordinis FF. Praedicatorum* (Ripoll et Bremond, 8 vols., Romae, 1729-1740), I, pp. 366, 370, 392 (hereafter cited: *Bull. Praed.*). Cf. Meersseman, Giles, "La Prédication Dominicaine dans Les Congrégations Mariales et Italie au XIIIe siècle," *Archivum Fratrum Praedicatorum,* XVIII (1948), p. 135. Cf. also *Bullarii Franciscani Epitome seu Summa Bullarum et Supplementum* (ed. Conrad Eubel, Quaracchi, 1908), n. 974 (hereafter cited: *Bull. Fran. Epit.*); *Bullarium Franciscanum Romanorum Pontificum* (Vols. I-IV, ed. Joanne Sbaraglea, Roma, 1759-1768; Vols. V-VII, ed. Conrad Eubel, Roma, 1898-1904), I, nn. 545, 1480 (hereafter cited: *Bull. Fran.*).

[43]For example, Alexander IV, under date of Nov. 8, 1257, bestows the following spiritual concession: "Rectoribus, confratribus, et sororibus universis fraternitatis b. Mariae . . . vere poenitentibus, qui venerint semel in mense ac diebus solemnibus ad congregationem, quam secundum statuta sua faciunt, ad missarum solemnia et ver-

undertaken by these confraternities were: the relief of the poor by alms, service to the sick by the founding and staffing of hospitals, the visiting of and administering to those in prison, the soliciting of alms for the building and repair of churches, the providing of dowries for young nubile women, and the caring of orphans and widows.[44]

The emergence of heresy in the 13th and 14th centuries and the resultant institution of the office of episcopal inquisition evoked another type of confraternity, whose express purpose was to assist the inquisitors in combatting heresy. Members of these confraternities were assigned the lay functions inherent in the trials and the carrying out of the sentences.[45] A number of penitential confraternities also appeared at this time, if not in direct imitation of the third orders, at least under the immediate influence of the penitential spirit of the Mendicants.[46]

According to particular law, the confraternity was established with the permission and consent of the Ordinary who had the duty of vigilance over its charitable works.[47] During the 12th and 13th centuries the confraternity took on the juridical form of the corporate or organic body, possessing property and administering funds under ecclesiastical supervision. Synodal laws at this time uniformly asserted the right of the Church to institute associations and oversee the administration of temporalities insofar as they were ecclesiastical organizations.[48] Confraternities attached to the churches or convents of religious orders were often placed under their direct supervision and administration. As a result,

---

bum Dei audienda, 100 dies de iniuncta eis poenitentia relaxat."—*Bull. Fran. Epit.*, n. 974.

[44]Cf. *Bull. Fran.*, I, nn. 141, 245, 545, 612, 712, 870, 1480, 1512; II, nn. 69, 527, 578, 593, 844, 847, 880, 941, 1216, 1387, 1707; III, nn. 78, 133, 352, 713, 725, 869, 1033, 1229, 1277, 1308.

[45]Cf. Meersseman, G., "La Confréries de Sainte Dominique," *Archivum Fratrum Praedicatorum*, XX (1950), pp. 5-113 and "Les Confréries de Saint-Pierre Martyr," *Archivum Fratrum Praedicatorum*, XXI (1951), pp. 51-196, in which are sketched the historical development of the various types of confraternities set up under Dominican influence to aid in the suppression of heresy.

[46]*Bull. Fran.*, I, 870, 1480, etc. Meersseman, G., *art. cit.*, XX (1950), p. 31 ff.; and XXI (1951), p. 51 ff. where the penitential confraternities of St. Peter the Martyr are expressly considered.

[47]Cf. page 11, above.

[48]Council of Arles (1234)—Mansi, XXIII, 339; Council of Cognac (1238)—Mansi, XXIII, 494; Council of Bordeaux (1255)—Mansi, XXIII, 865-866.

the religious superior together with two or three other community members formed the administrative board.[49]

It should be remarked here that the history of ecclesiastical societies reveals the most fluid lines of organization and the most diversified compass of activity. For the most part, the particular enactments of synods and councils reiterate the right of the Church to establish ecclesiastical societies and to regulate the administration of their holdings. Far from imposing uniform legislation with a view to regimenting their internal government, the Church permitted the founders of these societies to formulate the norms which guarded and guided their interior life and external activities. Hence, almost without exception, these associations had their own particular statutory laws, in which detailed provisions were made for: the election of officers, the common prayers, the frequency of reception of the sacraments of Penance and Holy Communion, the number of Masses to be offered for deceased members, liturgical obligations (e.g., processions), the corporal works of mercy peculiar to the association, alms-gathering, and the management of funds.[50]

The Council of Trent promulgated the first piece of general legislation concerning ecclesiastical societies of laymen. In session 22 the Council Fathers clearly underscored the right of the Church, and in particular the duty of the Bishop in his diocese, to supervise religious activities. The point was vigorously made that Bishops have the right to visitate any and all kinds of associations and confraternities of the laity.[51] In its next chapter the Council prescribed that the ecclesiastical and lay administrators of confraternities submit to the local Ordinary an annual financial report on the administration of the confraternity's funds and the distribution of alms donated by the faithful.[52] This measure provided

[49]*Bull. Praed.*, III, p. 131; *Bull. Fran.*, III, n. 1229; *Bullarium Carmelitanum plures complectens Summorum Pontificum Constitutiones ad Ordinem Fratrum Beatissimae Dei Genitricis de Monte Carmelo spectantes* (2 vols., Romae, 1715-1768), I, p. 224 (hereafter cited: *Bull. Carm.*).

[50]Cf. Durand, H., "Confrérie," *Dictionnaire de Droit Canonique* (ed. R. Naz, Paris: Librairie Letouzey et Ané, 1935—), IV, col. 146 (hereafter cited: *DDC*); Le Bras, G., "Les Confréries," *RHDFE*, XIX (1940-1941), p. 332 ff.

[51]Conc. Trident., sess. XXII, *de ref.*, c. 8: "Episcopi . . . habeant jus visitandi hospitalia, collegia quaecunque ac confraternitates laicorum . . ."—*Canones et Decreta Sacrosancti Oecumenici Concilii Tridentini* (Romae: ex typographia polyglotta S. C. de Propaganda Fide, 1882).

[52]Conc. Trident., sess. XXII, *de ref.*, c. 9: "Administratores tam ecclesiastici

a general check on the various types of associations and in particular narrowed the margin of likelihood that abuses might undermine the effectiveness of their varied activities. At the same time, the religious enthusiasm and devotion of the laity were efficiently channeled under episcopal authority, principally by means of personal or delegated visitation of their churches and chapels. Since the Bishop's consent was necessary to institute an ecclesiastical society and his approval of the statutes mandatory, the religious activities of the members of the society were subject to close and continual observation. The immediate objects of episcopal supervision were: the recitation of public prayers, the modalities of religious processions, the practice of public and private penance. All of these, needless to add, were provided for in some measure in their statutory law.[53] To be sure, the Council of Trent in general restated synodal legislation which had been in effect since the 12th century. This, in most cases, had proven adequate. However, an important historical phenomenon elicited due consideration. The 14th and 15th centuries had witnessed the widespread growth of similarly structured ecclesiastical societies, founded for the same purpose and bearing the same generic designation, but now under the auspices of Religious Orders and associated by varying degrees of affiliation to the communities of these same orders. In addition, numerous privileges and a variety of indulgences had been obtained from the Holy See in behalf of the members of these societies at the instance of Religious Superiors.[54] As a result, there was a perceptible need for uniform, general legislation to guide Religious Superiors both in the establishment of associations and in the communication of privileges.

Article 5: Archconfraternities and Primary Associations

If the religious climate of the 13th and 14th centuries fostered the upsurge of ecclesiastical societies to meet the challenge of rampant heresies, the ecclesiological clashes of the 16th century encouraged no less

---

quam laici fabricae cujusvis ecclesiae, etiam cathedralis, hospitalis, confraternitatis, eleemosynae, montis pietatis et quorumcunque piorum locorum, singulis annis teneantur reddere rationem administrationis ordinario."

[53]Cf. Le Bras, G., "Les Confréries," *RHDFE*, XIV (1940-1941), p. 337.

[54]Cf. Meersseman, G., "Les Confréries de Sainte Dominique," *Archivum Fratrum Praedicatorum*, XXI (1951), p. 69 ff. Consult also *Bull. Fran. Epit.*, n. 974 and

energetic an expression of orthodox solidarity. Uncounted groups of the laity crystallized their reaction against Protestantism by uniting together in special kinds of associations. Because of the great need for individual religious instruction, the Confraternity of Christian Doctrine was organized at this time with headquarters in Rome.[55] The effects of heresies directed against the Holy Eucharist were offset by innumerable confraternities in honor of the Blessed Sacrament. The principal one of this type was attached to the Church of Santa Maria sopra Minerva in Rome.[56] The traditional devotion of Catholicism to the Blessed Virgin Mary and the saints was made the target of relentless heretical attacks. But these were countered by the establishment of flourishing Marian sodalities and congregations, in large measure under the direction of the newly founded Society of Jesus.[57]

As the number and influence of the associations continued to grow, it became inevitable that a movement towards coordination, at least for those sharing a similar title and purpose, should gain momentum. In fact, attempts at coordination soon veered in the direction of centralization, a trend that resulted in the establishment of primary societies and archconfraternities. The driving force behind this movement for unification was generated by the religious orders and congregations, themselves continually growing and thereby achieving successive degrees of awareness of the solidarity that only centralization brings. As the religious institutes expanded numerically and geographically and their common problems with civil authority grew in proportion, it became increasingly clear that an effective solution to their difficulties lay in an active society of strong clients and influential patrons, who could and would argue their case. By the same token, associations found that affiliation with religious orders and congregations was a fruitful source of spiritual advantages. With the increase of incentives for joining, interest in the associations grew, membership multiplied, influence intensified. The expansion of associations elicited the granting of more extensive

---

footnote 1; *Bull. Fran., I,* nn. 141, 245, 545, etc.; *Bullarium Ordinis Eremitorum S. Augustini* (Romae, 1628), pp. 65, 209 (hereafter cited: *BOE S. Aug.*).

[55]S. Pius V, const. *"Ex debito,"* 6 oct. 1571—*Bull. Rom. Taur.*, VII, p. 945.

[56]Paul III, const. *"Dominus noster,"* 30 nov. 1539—*Bull. Rom. Taur.*, VI, p. 275.

[57]Gregory XIII, const. *"Omnipotentis Dei,"* 5 dec. 1584—*Bull. Rom. Taur.*, VIII, p. 499. Cf. Duhr, J., "La Confrérie," *RHE,* XXXV1 (1939), p. 470; Le Bras, G., "Les Confréres," *RHDFE,* pp. 325-326.

privileges and richer indulgences. Specific requests were directed to the Holy See by Religious Superiors, who petitioned the faculty to communicate to recently established associations privileges that had been granted and were already in effect in other associations set up by the same religious.[58] In many cases the Holy See granted to a religious order the power to communicate privileges through its confraternity in Rome to those founded by the same order outside of Rome.[59]

With this remarkable growth of identical associations throughout the world and the ensuing communication of indulgences, it was only a matter of time before each specifically different society established in Rome came to be considered the archetype of its group. Such, then, was the origin of the primary society and the archconfraternity. Given these circumstances, original grants of privileges and indulgences by the Holy See to the primary society situated in Rome were, with apostolic permission, communicated to its affiliates. This communication procedure enabled the Holy See to maintain a direct vigilance over the various kinds of privileges and indulgences enjoyed by the far-flung associations. Immediate control over the spiritual privileges of the primary association in Rome brought with it an indirect but effective control over the spiritual privileges of the affiliated associations.

Papal authorization was made a condition for conferring upon an association the title of primary association and the faculty to communicate privileges and indulgences. During the 16th century a number of Roman associations attained a double prerogative: the title of primary association, and the privilege to affiliate to itself other associations with authorization to communicate its indulgences. Although Leo X (1513-1521) and Paul III (1534-1549)[60] had established archconfraternities in Rome somewhat earlier, it was Gregory XIII (1572-1585) who gave impetus to the movement by extending this latter privilege to many Roman confraternities. During his pontificate the archconfraternities and primary societies in Rome were endowed with many privileges and

[58]Thus, as early as 1257, Alexander IV bestowed upon the confraternity set up by the Franciscans in Bagnorea (in the province of Rome), an indulgence which was subsequently communicated to a number of other confraternities established in other cities.—*Bull. Fran. Epit.*, n. 974.

[59]Cf. the preceding three footnotes.

[60]Leo X, const. "*Illius,*" 28 ian. 1520—*Bull. Rom. Taur.*, V, p. 739; Paul III, const. "*Altitudo,*" 7 febr. 1541—*Bull. Rom. Taur.*, VI, p. 306.

indulgences, in addition to the faculty to communicate them to their affiliates.[61]

[61]Cf. *Bull. Rom. Taur.*, VIII, pp. 50, 264, 369, 530, 534. In his official acts Gregory XIII refers to a confraternity, the *Societas Recommendatorum Beatae Mariae Virginis* (later known as *Gonfalonis*), founded in Rome in 1264, for which St. Bonaventure had arranged a formulary of prayers. Considered by some the oldest confraternity in Rome, this organization is believed to have achieved the status of archconfraternity in 1270.—*Bull. Rom. Taur.*, VIII, pp. 145 and 373. Sixtus V (1585-1590) favored this archconfraternity with many privileges and faculties—*Bull. Rom. Taur.*, VIII, pp. 673, 681 and 726. Cf. Borkowski, Aurelius L., *De Confraternitatibus Ecclesiasticis*, The Catholic University of America Canon Law Studies, n. 3 (Washingtonii: Universitas Catholica Americae, 1918), p. 19.

CHAPTER II

COMMON LAW AND THE PRIMARY SOCIETIES

Article 1: "Quaecumque" of Clement VIII (1592-1605)

The most important and comprehensive legislation concerning archconfraternities and primary societies prior to the Code of Canon Law is represented by the constitution of Clement VIII, *Quaecumque,* published on December 7, 1604.[1] This constitution was issued to check certain abuses in the establishment and affiliation of ecclesiastical associations. Many religious orders and several primary societies had been authorized not only to affiliate already existing societies and to communicate privileges to them, but also to establish new associations.[2] In many cases the formalities of establishing and affiliating associations as prescribed in the Apostolic Indult were not being observed. The absence of a set form frequently made the communication of indulgences tenuous, thus surrounding the gaining of indulgences with all kinds of uncertainties. At times fees were exacted for affiliation, so that the concomitant communication of indulgences and spiritual favors was not without the appearance of simony. It was against such abuses that the *Quaecumque* of Clement VIII was primarily directed.[3]

This Apostolic Constitution, it may be noted in passing, did not affect the power of Bishops in this matter.[4] The subjects directly affected by this legislation were orders of regulars, religious institutes, archconfraternities and other primary societies, congregations and all

[1] *Codicis Iuris Canonici Fontes cura Emi Petri Card. Gasparri editi* (9 vols., Romae [later Civitate Vaticana]: Typis Polyglottis Vaticanis, 1923-1939; Vols. VII-IX ed. *cura et studio Emi Justiniani Card. Seredi*), n. 192 (hereafter cited: *Fontes*). The only other piece of general legislation relating to primary societies was the *Exposcit* of Gregory XIII, dated July 15, 1583, which dealt with precedence among ecclesiastical associations. The prescriptions of this document will be considered in chapter VI.—*Fontes,* n. 151.

[2] *Bull. Rom. Taur.,* VIII, pp. 50, 530, 630, 659.

[3] Cf. *Quaecumque:* par. 1 and 2—*Fontes,* n. 192.

[4] Bishops acting with delegated or ordinary power could validly establish an eccle-

ecclesiastical associations affiliated to them. Only those ecclesiastical societies founded by episcopal authority fell beyond the scope of this legislative measure. Hence, Clement VIII in no way curtailed or altered episcopal or synodal regulations dealing with ecclesiastical associations established by the local Ordinary.

Since the *Quaecumque* serves as the basis for later legislation and decisions on the part of the Holy See, a detailed analysis of its various provisions affecting ecclesiastical associations is in order.

1) The Constitution required for validity that there be established in the churches of regulars and seculars only one association having the same nature and title. The establishment of this association required the consent of the local Ordinary and the obtaining of testimonial letters from him.

2) For the affiliation of ecclesiastical societies to a primary society the following provisions were demanded for validity:

a) The archconfraternity or affiliating society had to secure an Apostolic Indult. No archconfraternity or primary society could affiliate other ecclesiastical societies except by authorization of the Holy See.[5]

b) The affiliating archconfraternity or primary society could affiliate only one association in the same town, city, or locality.[6]

c) The association seeking affiliation could not already have been affiliated to another archconfraternity or affiliating institute of any kind; furthermore, the association to be affiliated must have been validly established by episcopal or papal authority.[7]

3) With regard to the communication of indulgences ensuing upon affiliation, only those privileges and indulgences were communicated which had been granted to the affiliating order or primary society specifically and by name. Thus, the actual communication of privi-

---

siastical society by any particular form of authentic decree, without being held to the prescriptions of the *Quaecumque*. Cf. S. C. Indulg., *Cameracen.*, 25 ian. 1842, ad 4—*Fontes*, n. 5022.

[5]If a primary society was granted the faculty to affiliate, the Holy See made specific reference to this fact in the Apostolic Indult. At times some confraternities were raised to the status of archconfraternity, but the power to affiliate was withheld. Cf. Paul III, 7 febr. 1541—*Bull. Rom. Taur.*, VI, p. 306.

[6]Cf. S. C. Ep. et Reg., *Taurinen.*, 20 dec. 1594—*Fontes*, n. 1525.

[7]Cf. *Bull. Rom. Taur.*, X, p. 80.

leges was restricted to those directly and expressly granted by the Holy See. Any privileges acquired by the primary society indirectly (e.g., through a prior communication from another affiliating society) were not communicable to its affiliates.

4) An approved formulary was to be followed in the affiliation of associations.[8]

5) For the publication of communicated indulgences, privileges, and indults, the previous recognition of the local Ordinary and two capitulars was necessary. The summary list of the communicated privileges and indulgences was to be submitted to the local Ordinary. He, together with the two capitulars, was to examine the papal documents granting the privileges and indulgences and to authenticate the list.[9]

6) Letters formulated for the establishment and affiliation of ecclesiastical associations were to be issued *gratis*. An offering, even if spontaneously made on these occasions, was not to be accepted.[10]

The validity of every affiliation was conditioned by the provisions of the *Quaecumque*. A penalty reserved to the Holy See was leveled against anyone presuming to act contrary to its prescriptions. The Constitution was to be put into effect in Europe within a year and beyond the continent within two years.[11]

The primary purpose of Clement VIII's Constitution was to bring the activity of archconfraternities and affiliating institutes under closer

[8]The formulary was drawn up by the Sacred Congregation of Indulgences (1604) and approved by Pope Clement VIII. For a copy of this formulary cf. L. Ferraris, *Prompta Bibliotheca, Canonica, Iuridica, Moralis, Theologica necnon Ascetica, Polemica, Rubricistica, Historica* (9 vols., Romae, 1885-1899), s.v., "Confraternitas," art. 1, nn. 17-18 (hereafter cited: *Bibliotheca*).

[9]This had already been demanded by the Council of Trent. Cf. Conc. Trident., sess. XXI, *de ref.*, c. 9.

[10]Cf. *BOE S. Aug.*, p. 134; *Bull. Rom. Taur.*, VIII, p. 50.

[11]Among other provisions affecting ecclesiastical societies, the *Quaecumque* reminded the officials that the particular statutes of each association were to be examined and approved by the local Ordinary, and that they remained subject to his correction. Moreover, the local Ordinary alone possessed the right to authorize the collecting of alms and to determine the circumstances of such collections. The use of coin boxes and money baskets in the oratories and chapels of the associations was expressly forbidden. The offerings were to be used for the repair of churches, chapels, and for the specific works proper to the society. Cf. *Bull. Carm.*, I, pp. 474, 500; *Bull. Fran.*, III, n. 1277; S. C. C., *Ariminen.*, 29 aug. 1595—*Fontes*, n. 2291.

ecclesiastical supervision. Two reasons made this imperative: first, the nature of affiliation with its consequent communication of privileges and indulgences necessitated episcopal vigilance; second, the numerous affiliations made by religious superiors and the officials of primary societies called for some standards of uniformity. During the 15th and 16th centuries, confraternities spread throughout the Church with such speed and in such numbers that the Holy See recognized the need for control measures. The number of qualified persons possessing the faculty to establish associations and the system of communicating privileges and indulgences presented an overly complex and confusing pattern of affairs. For example, it was not at all unusual for an individual parish to have an excessive number of ecclesiastical associations. While some societies had their own particular church or oratory, others had their own special altar or chapel in the parish church. In some instances, the chapel of the society was distinct from the church of a religious community or externally connected to it; in other cases, a society possessed an altar or chapel in the church of an exempt religious institute. In one case, the pastor was the moderator of a society, while in another, the society itself provided a benefice whose incumbent was its chaplain or moderator.[12]

The *Quaecumque* of Clement VIII tried to restore order to this welter of confusion by standardizing the disparate practices on the part of religious superiors and primary societies. In demanding the consent of the local Ordinary for the establishment of an ecclesiastical association, and placing the examination, approval, and correction of the statutes in his hands, the Constitution directly submitted every association to episcopal control. The administration of funds, the liturgical ceremonies, the works of charity had already been subjected to his vigilance in virtue of the legislation of the Council of Trent.[13] The effect of the *Quaecumque* was to strengthen the power of the local Ordinary over the internal life of the association. By controlling the further communication of privileges and indulgences, by setting a definite limit to the duplication of associations in the same locality, Clement VIII placed a necessary curb on the independence of ecclesiastical associations without stifling their religious spirit and zeal.

[12]Cf. footnotes on page 13.

[13]Conc. Trident., sess. XXII, *de ref.*, cc. 8-9.

ARTICLE 2: FROM THE "QUAECUMQUE" TO THE CODE OF CANON LAW

After Pope Clement VIII's *Quaecumque* (1604), no subsequent piece of general legislation affecting primary societies was enacted until the Code of Canon Law. The approved formulary for the act of affiliation was issued by the Sacred Congregation of Indulgences and each primary society was bound to use the set formula under pain of nullity.[14] Pope Paul V (1605-1621) left no room for doubt as to the importance of the formulary of affiliation. His Constitution *Quae salubriter* admonished the moderators of primary societies that the formulary of his predecessor was a condition for the valid communication of indulgences. Any act posited in contravention to its prescription was rendered null and void.[15] Nevertheless, in 1671, the Sacred Congregation of Indulgences again had to remind officials of primary societies and supreme moderators of other affiliating institutes of the necessity of observing all the prescriptions of the *Quaecumque*. None of them might be omitted without affecting validity.[16]

By the middle of the 17th century, the great number and extensive activities of ecclesiastical associations made it imperative to define clearly the relationship between the parish and ecclesiastical associations within the parish unit itself. Many parishes at this time had several ecclesiastical societies within their boundaries, some with their own churches and oratories distinct and separate from the parish plants, others with chapels in or connected to the parish buildings. Furthermore, in 1676, the Sacred Congregation of Indulgences exhorted each parish to establish a confraternity of the Blessed Sacrament to promote greater devotion to the Holy Eucharist among the laity.[17] Moreover, many local Ordinaries had already established the confraternity of Christian Doctrine in their dioceses, to aid in the religious education of the children.[18]

Such an overlapping of ecclesiastical societies within a single parish could not but occasion many and varied disputes. Numerous replies from the Sacred Congregations reflect the intraparochial problems of the 17th and 18th centuries. In general, these responses from the Holy

[14]Ferraris, L., *Bibliotheca,* s.v., "Confraternitas," art. 1, n. 18.

[15]Paul V, const. "*Quae salubriter,*" 3 nov. 1610—*Fontes,* n. 196.

[16]S. C. Indulg., 19 mart. 1671—*Fontes,* n. 4946.

[17]S. C. Indulg., 23 apr. 1676—*Fontes,* n. 4948.

[18]St. Pius V, const. "*Ex debito,*" 6 oct. 1571—*Fontes,* n. 141.

See deal with the rights and obligations of ecclesiastical associations in relationship to the local Ordinary and to the pastor. Repeatedly the Sacred Congregations insist that the local Ordinary exercise his full complement of rights.[19] As for the association's dependence upon the pastor, the Sacred Congregations clarified the relationship between the pastor on the one hand and the association with its chaplain on the other. A number of decrees offer detailed lists of liturgical services to be considered nonparochial functions, decide when and where processions may be held, vindicate the right of societies to hold meetings in accord with approved statutes and to dispose of their own goods without the intervention of the pastor.[20]

Prior to the *Quaecumque,* the question of precedence among ecclesiastical associations had been settled by the Constitution *Exposcit* (July 15, 1583) of Gregory XIII (1572-1585).[21] The Constitution set down two principles as general law to decide which confraternity had the right of precedence. The first rule related to the antiquity of the association: that which had been established first in the locality was considered to have the right.[22] If a doubt still remained, the second principle had application: that association which had been the first to use a distinctive garb or habit was to have the right of precedence.[23] Although these two principles were somewhat modified by the pre-eminent right of precedence awarded to confraternities of the Blessed Sacrament,[24] they served as the basis for the many decisions of the Sacred Congregations concerning precedence prior to the Code of Canon Law.

[19]These episcopal powers included: the right to establish associations, the right to approve their statutes, vigilance over the administration of funds, supervision over public worship, and the right to preside at elections of the officials of ecclesiastical societies.—*Fontes,* nn. 1824, 3079, 3093, 3293, 4978; *ASS,* XII (1879), 17; XIII (1880), 127.

[20]Cf. especially: S. R. C., *Urbis et Orbis,* 12 ian. 1704—*Fontes,* n. 5733; *Placentina,* 22 nov. 1710—*Fontes,* n. 5746; *Perusina,* 9 iul. 1718—*Fontes,* n. 5757. Consult also *ASS,* I (1865), 582; VI (1870), 109.

[21]*Fontes,* n. 151.

[22]"Qui in quasi-possessione praecedentiae ac iuris."

[23]"Ii qui prius saccis usi sunt."

[24]S. R. C., *Vercellen.,* 18 iun. 1695—*Fontes,* n. 5697.

Article 3: Decrees of the Sacred Congregations Concerning Primary Societies

After the publication of the *Quaecumque* of Clement VIII, the Sacred Congregations dealt with numerous cases of affiliation of associations to primary societies and the communication of privileges and indulgences. Authentic decisions issued throughout the 17th and 18th centuries insist on the observance of the prescriptions of the *Quaecumque*. Periodically the Roman Congregations pointed out that the Clementine Constitution was binding on all primary societies and that all the norms were to be followed under pain of nullity.[25]

On January 8, 1861, the Sacred Congregation of Indulgences issued a very important decree for ecclesiastical associations.[26] This document extended a general sanation to all invalidly constituted ecclesiastical societies and also validated all affiliations and all communications of indulgences attempted in violation of the provisions of the *Quaecumque*. The Sacred Congregation took cognizance of the many invalid affiliations owing to the illegal procedures on the part of the officials of the primary societies. In response to the many petitions and requests directed to the Holy See for validation Pius IX granted the sanation.

The last important pre-Code legislative measure affecting primary societies was issued on October 19, 1866. The Sacred Congregation of Indulgences published a general decree which both renewed and complemented the prescriptions of the *Quaecumque*.[27] It contained two formularies to be observed by the superiors of affiliating societies. Each formulary had to be used by the respective affiliating societies and observed at least in its basic form.[28] The first formulary was to be used by religious superiors in establishing associations and communicating privileges to them. The second concerned the faculty of the primary society to affiliate and embodied an exemplar to be used in effecting that act. Textually, the latter formulary recalled the juridical dispositions of

[25]Cf. S. C. Indulg., 23 apr. 1676—*Fontes*, n. 4948; *Romana*, 22 dec. 1710—*Fontes*, n. 4952; 10 apr. 1720—*Fontes*, n. 4960; *Urbis*, 31 iul. 1756—*Fontes*, n. 4981; S. C. C., *Potentina*, 29 maii 1683—*Fontes*, n. 2869; *Novarien.*, 3 et 24 sept. 1718—*Fontes*, n. 3174; S. R. C., *Posnanien.*, 7 dec. 1658—*Fontes*, n. 5512; *Veneta*, 14 nov. 1676—*Fontes*, n. 5615.

[26]*Fontes*, n. 5061.

[27]*Fontes*, n. 5074.

[28]"Formula servanda saltem in substantialibus . . ."

the *Quaecumque* of Clement VIII and again reminded the moderators of primary societies that all those dispositions were not only in force but still requisite for valid affiliation. Thus, to eliminate doubts and discrepancies on the part of those drawing up the documents of affiliation, the text of this second formulary embodied a list of the essential requirements for affiliation. The formulary also required for validity that the document contain a specific enumeration of privileges and indulgences to be communicated to the affiliates, so as to eliminate the possibility of error in so important a matter. Insistence on a detailed formulary afforded the moderators of affiliating societies a safe and certain guide. Most important of all, this decree was particularly timely since the privilege of affiliation was being ever more frequently granted during the 19th century.[29]

Another juridical element not explicitly found in the *Quaecumque* of Clement VIII or in the decree of the Sacred Congregation of Indulgences of 1866 was the condition requiring the primary society and its affiliate to have the same title and the same purpose. This requirement of identity of title and purpose was strongly insisted upon by Innocent XI (1676-1689) as a formality for the granting of affiliation.[30] From the latter part of the 17th century to the publication of the formulary of the Sacred Congregation (1866), the Holy See made it a condition for valid affiliation that associations bear the same official title as the primary society, and be similar in nature, unless the apostolic indult expressly granted the primary society special jurisdiction in this regard.[31] As a result, the decree of the Sacred Congregation of Indulgences of

[29]Throughout the 19th century there was a general resurgence of all ecclesiastical associations, following a sharp decline in the previous century. The efforts of Pius IX and Leo XIII infused new vitality into ecclesiastical societies, so that on the eve of the publication of the Code of Canon Law ecclesiastical associations enjoyed a period of great vigor and influence. Cf. S. C. Indulg., *Urbis et Orbis,* 5 aug. 1851—*Fontes,* n. 5045; Leo XIII, ep. encycl. "*Etsi Nos,*" 15 febr. 1882—*Fontes,* n. 583.

[30]Innocentius XI, const. "*Cum nos,*" 11 maii 1689—*Bull. Rom. Taur.,* XIX, p. 930.

[31]Cf. S. C. Indulg., *Papien.,* 20 iul. 1728—*Fontes,* n. 4964; *Utinen.,* 9 dec. 1862—*ASS,* II (1866), 534; *Albien.,* 17 iul. 1891—*Fontes,* n. 5112; S. C. C., *Maceraten.,* ad 2, 24 mart. 1736 et 17 maii 1737—Zamboni, *Collectio declarationum S. Congr. cardinal. Sacr. Conc. Trident. interpret.* (4 vols., Atrebati apud Rousseau—Leroy, 1860-1868), III, v°, "Sodalitium," §7, n. 68.

1866 incorporated this condition into the text of the document for affiliation.[32]

The decree also demanded that the primary society enclose a complete list of communicated indulgences and privileges in its official instrument of affiliation. According to the prescriptions of the *Quaecumque*[33] and the decree,[34] only those privileges and indulgences that had been granted to the primary society directly and specifically by the Holy See were subject to communication. Privileges and indulgences which the primary society had itself acquired through communication were not included. Because the Holy See desired absolute certainty in this matter, it demanded presentation of a complete list of only those communicable privileges and indulgences whose possession by direct grant the primary society could prove. Furthermore, this list had to be acknowledged officially by the local Ordinary.[35]

Shortly after the publication of the Clementine *Quaecumque,* the Sacred Congregation of Indulgences revoked by decree all indulgences granted to primary societies by the Holy See prior to November 3, 1610.[36] This revocation was motivated by the fact that many doubts had arisen concerning the concessions of indulgences to affiliating societies. Such, in fact, was the state of confusion in the communication of indulgences to affiliates, that the Sacred Congregation regarded a complete revocation of all existing concessions from the Holy See as the

[32]S. C. Indulg., 19 oct. 1866—*Fontes,* n. 5074. The prescribed formulary reads: "..., libenter nostrae Archiconfraternitati *alias eiusdem instituti Confraternitates* adiungimus et aggregamus, ..." In listing the necessary conditions for affiliation the text continues: "... 1. Quod *unica* tantum *Confraternitas ejusdem instituti et generis* institui et aggregari possit in ecclesiis tam saecularium quam Regularium" (italics supplied). Cf. Amanieu, A., "Archiconfrérie," *DDC,* I, col. 936, 4°. Sixtus V (1585-1590) granted an archconfraternity the express faculty to affiliate confraternities with a different title as long as these had the same purpose as the archconfraternity.—*Bull. Rom. Taur.,* VIII, p. 744. Cf. S. C. Indulg., *Utinen.,* 9 dec. 1862—*ASS,* II (1866), 534.

[33]Clement VIII, const. *"Quaecumque,"* 7 dec. 1604, §4—*Fontes,* n. 192.

[34]S. C. Indulg., 19 oct. 1866, II—*Fontes,* n. 5074.

[35]Conc. Trident., sess. XXI, *de ref.,* c. 9; Clement VIII, const. *"Quaecumque,"* 7 dec. 1604—*Fontes,* n. 192.

[36]S. C. Indulg., 19 mart. 1671—*Fontes,* n. 4946. This decree withdrew all indulgences granted prior to the *Quae salubriter* (Nov. 3, 1610) of Paul V, which the Holy See had not renewed or reconfirmed.

only workable solution. Thus, primary societies were forced to apply for a renewal of grants predating the constitution of Paul V.[37] If these concessions were neither renewed nor reconfirmed, they were to be considered null and void.

On March 7, 1678, the Sacred Congregation continued its work of resolving various doubts about papal concessions of indulgences by publishing a list of proscribed grants.[38] This list contained alleged grants of indulgences never actually made by the Holy See. The decree also cited a number of indulgences which, though granted by various Roman Pontiffs, had later been revoked. Others still were proscribed, because these grants, despite their temporary character, had come to be regarded as perpetual by their recipients. Furthermore, this list of revoked indulgences included all concessions effected through communication by a primary society prior to the *Quae salubriter* of Paul V, unless the communicated indulgences had received reconfirmation after the publication of the constitution. As a result, all affiliates after the publication of the *Quae salubriter* possessed communicated indulgences only in virtue of explicit renewal or authentic reconfirmation.

The Holy See consistently demanded that primary societies spare no efforts in observing the legal formalities attached to the communication of indulgences. In this connection, the detailed list of indulgences required by the formulary of 1866 served a twofold purpose. First, the primary society was assured that its possession of these indulgences would not be called into doubt, as all had been made by direct grant from the Holy See. Secondly, the affiliates would have a complete and certain enumeration of all indulgences received through communication.[39]

[37]"*Quae salubriter,*" 3 nov. 1610—*Fontes*, n. 196.

[38]*Fontes*, n. 4951.

[39]The Sacred Congregation always considered the instrument of affiliation absolutely essential. In a case brought before the Holy See in 1710, the Sacred Congregation of the Council would not recognize an affiliation because the original document of affiliation could not be produced. Cf. S. C. C., *Lancianen.*, 20 sept. 1710—*Fontes*, n. 3093; also consult S. C. Ep. et Reg., 6 febr. 1874—*ASS*, VII (1873-1874), 641.

Conclusion

The various norms of the *Quaecumque* of Clement VIII[40] and the additions made by the approved decree of the Sacred Congregation of Indulgences[41] represented the general law for primary societies until the Code of Canon Law came into effect. Those sections of canons 720-725 which treat specifically of primary societies are for the most part a renewal of this legislation. Both canon 722 (which deals with the communication of privileges and indulgences) and canon 723 (which treats the conditions for a valid affiliation) are a reenactment of the pre-Code law. According to the principle of interpretation enunciated in canon 6,[42] these canons are subject to the same interpretation given the pre-Code legislation. Therefore, because many authentic responses after the publication of the *Quaecumque* explained the norms of the constitution, the present law concerning primary societies will find its interpretation in them.

40*Fontes*, n. 192.

41S. C. Indulg., *Urbis et Orbis*, 8 ian. 1861—*Fontes*, n. 5061; 19 oct. 1866—*Fontes*, n. 5074.

42Canon 6, 2°: Canones qui ius vetus ex integro referunt, ex veteris iuris auctoritate, atque ideo ex receptis apud probatos auctores interpretationibus, sunt aestimandi.

PART TWO

CANONICAL COMMENTARY

CHAPTER III

PRELIMINARY CANONICAL NOTIONS

Article 1: The Purpose of the Present Study

The purpose of the canonical section of this dissertation is to examine the norms of the Code of Canon Law which apply to a particular class of ecclesiastical associations: namely, archconfraternities, archsodalities and primary unions. The nature, dignity, rights and privileges of these societies as set forth in the various relevant canons will be examined at full length.[1] Since a primary society usually has the power of affiliating similar societies and communicating its privileges and indulgences to them, a thorough discussion will of necessity include the concepts of affiliation and communication of privileges. Neither of these two concepts can be overlooked in any genuine attempt at formulating a clear and adequate notion of a primary society.[2]

Primary associations, it should be noted further, are subject to the canonical prescriptions governing all ecclesiastical associations. When a society in the Church is raised to the juridical status of primary society, it does not *ipso facto* become a new juridical entity nor achieve exemption from legislation common to other ecclesiastical societies. For example, a confraternity which is raised to the dignity of an archconfraternity does not lose its original nature. Not only, therefore, is it now bound by the legislation proper to archconfraternities, but it also remains subject to the legislation proper to confraternities. Even a summary treatment of these general norms relating to ecclesiastical societies would unduly extend the scope of this study, necessitating as it does a commentary upon all the canons of part 3 in the second book of the Code of Canon Law.[3] Consequently, the material object of this dissertation must of set purpose be limited to those canonical norms dealing specifically

1Canons 701, 720-725.

2Cf. canon 720.

3Canons 684-719.

with primary societies.[4]

Clarity of procedure urges that a definition of the various types of ecclesiastical societies and a division of them be offered by way of introduction. These preliminary discussions of the various classes of societies in the Church will help distinguish the primary society from all others and highlight its particular characteristics. Thus, this initial canonical chapter serves a double purpose. It will outline the different types of associations recognized by the Church together with their similarities and differences. It will provide an introduction to the canonical section proper to this dissertation by laying the groundwork for a better understanding of the juridical elements involved or implied.

Article 2: An Ecclesiastical Association Defined

The early ecclesiastical associations of the faithful were designated by disparate, generic titles. In conciliar law especially, great flexibility characterized the terminology referring to ecclesiastical societies, so that it was extremely difficult, if not impossible, to distinguish the different classes of societies in the Church.[5] Even papal documents and pre-Code decrees of the Sacred Congregations were far from consistent in their wide range of titles for the different kinds of ecclesiastical associations.[6] In fact, the Code of Canon Law itself did not achieve a notable measure of uniformity in this matter.[7] Nor, finally, have the post-Code decrees of the Sacred Congregations employed technical terms exclusively when referring to specific kinds of ecclesiastical associations.[8]

[4]Canons 701, 720-725.

[5]This inconsistency of terminology is revealed by a cursory survey of conciliar legislation itself. Among the terms designating an ecclesiastical society one finds: *fratria, confratria, frateria, confraterna, colligatio, coniuratio, congregatio, confraternitas, collegius, schola, societas, sodalitas, charitas*. Cf. Ferraris, L., *Bibliotheca*, s.v., "Confraternitas," art. 1, n. 83. Cf. also the historical section of this dissertation.

[6]S. C. Ep. et Reg., *Romana*, 18 ian. 1907: "Porro vox confraternitatis in iure determinatum sensum non habet, quum etiam pro pia unione, congregatione et pio opere usurpatur."—*ASS*, XL (1907), 143. See also S. C. Indulg., *Urbis et Orbis*, 25 aug. 1897—*ASS*, XXX (1897), 276.

[7]By way of illustration, one might compare the use of the term, *sodalitas* in canon 702, §2 with that in canon 1356, §1; and *sodalitia* in canon 707 with that in canons 710, 720, and 913, 3o.

[8]S. C. C., *Corrienten.*, 13 nov. 1920: "Nota pariter divisio *confraternitatum* in

Under the generic phrase *association of the faithful* the Code of Canon Law includes various ecclesiastical societies which are distinct both from religious institutes and from societies of common life without public vows.[9] These ecclesiastical associations do not constitute a juridical state of perfection as Secular Institutes do,[10] yet they are truly ecclesiastical and must not be confused with secular (or nonecclesiastical) societies.[11]

Secular societies are those societies set up by private individuals without any authoritative act of establishment or approbation by the Church. The mere fact that these societies have a religious purpose and receive special recommendation from the Church does not constitute them a society established by ecclesiastical authority, or make them so approved as to endow them with the juridical status of ecclesiastical associations. Constituted as they are by nonecclesiastical authority, they remain nonecclesiastical in nature.[12]

Ecclesiastical associations, on the other hand, are societies of the faithful,[13] founded for a religious purpose and, in addition, either constituted a moral person by a decree of competent ecclesiastical authority, or awarded official approbation by the same competent authority. To establish a society so that it possesses ecclesiastical status depends upon a formal act of competent authority. This distinguishes ecclesiastical societies from secular or civil societies. In virtue of its ecclesiastical orientation, therefore, all activities proper to the society become subject in a particular way to the Church, whose approbation is the direct and immediate cause of its ecclesiastical status. Hence, in addition to the elements

---

laicales et *ecclesiasticas:* in qua divisione sumitur *confraternitas* pro qualibet societate seu associatione in finem pium inita, . . ."—*AAS,* XIII (1921), 139.

[9]Canon 685.

[10]Cf. Pius XII, const. "*Provida Mater Ecclesia,*" 2 febr. 1947—*AAS,* XXXIX (1948), 120.

[11]S. C. C., *Corrienten,* 13 nov. 1920—*AAS,* XIII (1921), 139. The expression *societas laica* is used by the Sacred Congregation to designate nonecclesiastical associations which are recommended by the Church. In rendering this expression into English the writer will use the word "secular" since it is closer in meaning than "lay."

[12]The St. Vincent de Paul Society is an example of a recommended secular society. Cf. S. C. C., *Corrienten.,* 13 nov. 1920—*AAS,* XIII (1921), 138.

[13]The term *faithful* is used in its broadest connotation, which includes cleric, religious, and layman. Cf. canon 693, §4.

necessary for any society, an ecclesiastical association requires the formal recognition of the Church. Without this authentic approbation, such a society (even though recommended) is not ecclesiastical.

The specific end or purpose of an ecclesiastical association must be religious in character.[14] The type of charitable works to which the society is devoted does not matter, provided only that they are religious in scope. The society may be primarily oriented to the sanctification of its members, as the third orders secular. On the other hand, it may have as its aim the promotion of public worship, as the Confraternity of the Blessed Sacrament. In any event, the purpose or aim of an ecclesiastical association must be essentially religious.[15]

Article 3: Division of Ecclesiastical Associations

Section 1: *Division According to Canonical Establishment*

In its formulation of the definition for an ecclesiastical association of the faithful, the Code of Canon Law provides for a twofold division on the basis of the nature of the jurisdictional act by which it is constituted. Thus there are:

1) associations which are established by competent ecclesiastical authority as moral persons. The constitution of a moral person in the Church always entails a formal act of establishment by proper authority. Only through this jurisdictional act can an association in the Church acquire moral personality, through which it becomes the subject of rights and obligations proper to ecclesiastical moral persons.[16]

2) associations which are approved by competent ecclesiastical authority although not established as moral persons. The second method of granting ecclesiastical recognition to an association is by way of simple approbation. This official approval by competent authority does not bestow juridical personality upon the society, but it does constitute special recognition and subjects it to a greater ecclesiastical vigilance than if merely recommended as a society. The necessity of this appro-

[14] Cf. canons 685 and 707.

[15] The canons deal only with ecclesiastical associations; they are not to be applied to secular societies. Cf. S. C. C., *Corrienten.*, 13 nov. 1920—*AAS*, XIII (1921), 138.

[16] Canons 685 and 100. Canons dealing with ecclesiastical moral persons must be applied to these associations, e.g., canons 101, 102, 1495, §2, 1557, §2, 2o, 1649.

bation is expressed in the general principle: no association is ecclesiastical unless it has at least approbation by competent authority. An association thus approved is recognized by the Church as capable of receiving spiritual privileges and favors, especially indulgences. Since this type of society lacks moral personality, it does not possess the rights and obligations proper to moral persons.[17]

Section 2: Division According to Juridical Nature and Structure

The canons divide ecclesiastical associations further by reason of the juridical nature and internal structure of a particular type of association. This classification includes:

1) *Third Order Secular.* In the words of the Code of Canon Law, a third order secular is an ecclesiastical society whose members, while living in the world under the direction and according to the spirit of a religious order, strive after greater Christian perfection in a manner consistent with secular life and in accordance with rules approved by the Holy See.[18] A third order secular is not a religious order as defined by canon 488. In this canon the term *order* designates a religious institute in which solemn vows are taken. On the other hand, the word *order* in the expression *third order secular* is used to set such an organization apart from other associations of the faithful, insofar as a third order secular makes profession of a definite rule of life, requires its members to undergo a novitiate and profession, and has for its primary purpose the commitment of its members to greater personal sanctification. Other ecclesiastical associations of the faithful do not have a rule, a novitiate or profession, and identify their primary purpose with the promotion of some charitable work.[19]

[17]Canon 708.

[18]Canon 702, §1.

[19]Although a third order secular immediately and primarily pledges its members to personal sanctification, an apostolate of charitable works is not thereby excluded. The new Constitution of the Third Order Secular of St. Francis reminds the tertiaries of the apostolate they have in the family and society, outlining the work they must perform in the promotion of vocations, assistance to the missions, participation in Catholic Action, propagation of good literature, etc. Cf. "Constitutiones Tertii Ordinis Saecularis Sancti Francisci Assisiensis," tit. III et IV, in *Tertius Ordo,* dec. 1957, p. 136 ff.

2) *Pious Union.* A pious union is an ecclesiastical association of the faithful, which does not have internal corporate structure and has as its direct and primary purpose the promotion of some form of apostolic activity.[20] Such an organization possesses the essential characteristics of an ecclesiastical society, namely, a religious purpose and ecclesiastical approbation, even though not established as a moral person. As to its purpose, it must in common with every ecclesiastical association be oriented to a spiritual objective, that is, it must be directed to and in conformity with the supernatural end of the Church. Hence, the term *religious purpose* is to be understood in its broadest connotation, so as to be applicable to a far-reaching variety of activities: among others, the promotion of personal sanctification, the fostering of divine worship and public cult, Catholic education, special devotion to the saints, a corporal or spiritual work of mercy.[21] The spiritual activities of the society are to be motivated by supernatural charity rather than mere philanthropy, since inherent in the notion of an ecclesiastical association is the element of subordination to the supernatural end of the Church.[22]

Pious unions may be canonically established as moral persons. In the absence of moral personality, they must at least be approved by competent authority as ecclesiastical societies.[23] In either case, however, whether canonically established as a moral person or not, such an association is not constituted after the manner of an organic body. For such organizational features would constitute it, in the technical terminology of the Code of Canon Law, a sodality.

3) *Sodality.* A sodality is, therefore, an ecclesiastical society whose inherent structure is modeled upon and determined after the manner

[20]Canon 707, §1.

[21]The *Association of the Holy Childhood,* the *Union of St. Anthony of Padua,* the *Union of Clerics for the Missions* are examples of pious unions. Cf. Seeberger, M., *Key to the Spiritual Treasures* (2. ed., Collegeville: St. Joseph's College, 1897); Beringer, F.-Steinen, P., *Die Ablaesse, ihr Wesen und Gebrauch* (2 vols., Paderborn: Ferdinand Schoeningh, 1921), II; Seraphinus de Angelis, *De Fidelium Associationibus* (2 vols., Neapoli: M. d'Auria, 1959), II.

[22]Cf. Michiels, G., *Principia Generalia de Personis in Ecclesia* (2. ed., Parisiis: Desclée, 1955), p. 384 (hereafter cited: *De Personis*).

[23]Canon 708.

of an organic body.[24] That is to say, by virtue of its internal hierarchical organization, the very government of the sodality through its president, councilors and other officers, directs and guides the common activity of the sodality and the administration of its temporal goods. The organic structure of a sodality is either prescribed by its statutory law or determined by the very nature of the sodality's religious activity. In either event, ecclesiastical approbation of the sodality extends to and includes its internal form of organization.[25]

Organic structure is essential to a sodality because it represents the specific difference which sets it apart from a pious union.[26] However, the concept of corporate structure poses a problem. The formulation of canon 707, §1 does not make it clear whether the expression "constituted after the manner of an organic body" includes moral personality.

Some authors explain that corporate structure necessarily includes moral personality, so that a sodality, technically speaking, must be established a moral person.[27] They argue that the internal hierarchical organization of a corporate body *ipso facto* demands moral per-

[24]Canon 707, §1. The wording of the canon is: ". . . si ad modum organici corporis sint constitutae, *sodalitia* audiunt." Canon 553 of the Oriental Code of Canon Law retains the same wording. Cf. Pius XII, litt. apost. *Cleri Sanctitati,* Motu Proprio Datae, 2 iun. 1957—*AAS,* XLIX (1957), 433-603 (hereafter cited: Motu Proprio *Cleri Sanctitati*).

[25]Cf. Vromant, G.-Bongaerts, L., *De Fidelium Associationibus* (2. ed., Bruges, Paris: Desclée de Brouwer, 1955), p. 100. Cf. also S. C. Indulg., *Urbis et Orbis,* 26 nov. 1880—*Fontes,* n. 5090. In this decree the Sacred Congregation distinguished ecclesiastical societies possessing organic structure from others possessing a less rigid or stabilized type of organization. The Sacred Congregation noted that societies which come close to a corporate organization in structure usually have a form of enrollment identified with a more or less solemn rite of public petition by and presentation of candidates, a period of probation and novitiate, or at least a reception signified by the conferral of some external insignia or emblem of membership (e.g., a scapular or medal). While not essential characteristics of corporate organization, these features may serve as positive indications thereof. The expression *ad modum organici corporis* points up the absolute requirement of a type of organization which enables the sodality to act as a corporate unit in and through this internal structure. Cf. Durand, H., "Confrérie," *DDC,* IV, col. 132.

[26]Canon 707, §1.

[27]Regatillo, E., *Institutiones Iuris Canonici* (5. ed., 2 vols., Santander: Editorial Sal Terrae, 1956), I, n. 782; Seraphinus de Angelis, *De Fidelium Associationibus,* I, p. 55; Vromant, G.-Bongaerts, L., *De Fidelium Associationibus,* p. 100; Matthaeus

sonality. Moreover, before the Code of Canon Law the organic structure of an ecclesiastical society was the distinctive feature of a confraternity, and confraternities were always moral persons.[28]

Other authors maintain that the corporate structure of a sodality does not necessarily postulate its establishment as a moral personality.[29] They agree that canon 707 does not clearly stipulate such a condition, but they argue that such an inference is warranted by a consistent interpretation of the canons of the Code of Canon Law referring to ecclesiastical societies. For example, canon 708 points out that confraternities must be established as moral persons, while pious unions need only the simple approbation of ecclesiastical authority. A sodality is a type of pious union, and therefore ecclesiastical approbation would be sufficient for its establishment.

Moreover, canons 553 and 554 of the Oriental Code of Canon Law repeat the wording of the corresponding canons (707 and 708) of the Latin Code. It is difficult to see why the legislator should mention expressly that confraternities are to be established as moral persons if this formality is already required by reason of their corporate structure. Again, if the legislator deemed it necessary to mention that a confraternity must be a moral person, why did he not do so for sodalities?

Still another argument may be drawn from an additional comparison between the Codes of the Latin and of the Oriental Churches. For the enrollment of a member into an association, canon 694, §2 of the Latin Code prescribes that his name be entered in the official register. Whenever an association is a moral person, the inscription of the name is a condition for valid enrollment.[30] Canon 542, §2 of

---

a Coronata, *Institutiones Iuris Canonici* (4. ed., 5 vols., Taurini: Marietti, 1950-1956), I, p. 920.

[28]Regatillo, E., *Institutiones Iuris Canonici,* I, n. 782. Cf. S. C. C., nov. 10, 1910—*AAS,* III (1911), 390.

[29]Wernz, F.-Vidal, P., *Ius Canonicum* (7 vols., Romae: Universitas Gregoriana, 1923-1938), III (*De Religiosis*), p. 525, nota (47); Beringer, F.-Steinen, P., *Die Ablaesse,* II, n. 42; De Meester, A., *Iuris Canonici et Iuris Canonici Civilis Compendium* (3 vols. in 4, Brugis: Desclée, 1921-1928), II, n. 1087; Sipos, S., *Enchiridion Iuris Canonici* (6. ed., Romae: Herder, 1954), pp. 352, 357. Matthaeus a Coronata, *Institutiones,* I, p. 885.

[30]Canon 694, §2: "Ut autem de receptione constet, inscriptio in albo associationis

the Oriental Code of Canon Law prescribes a similar enrollment. However, this entry of the name in the official register of the association is necessary for valid enrollment only in the case of an association which is a moral person *and* constituted after the manner of an organic body.[31] Here the legislator clearly distinguishes between moral personality and corporate structure. According to the wording of the canon, an association which is constituted a moral person does not necessarily demand corporate structure. Conversely, an association having corporate structure is not necessarily a moral person. If the phrase "constituted after the manner of an organic body" necessarily included the concept of moral personality, there would be no reason for its explicit mention in this canon.[32]

4) *Confraternity.* The fourth kind of ecclesiastical association belonging to this category based on internal structure is the confraternity. Its definition is found in canon 707, §2: a confraternity is a sodality that is set up as a moral person and has as its purpose the promotion of public worship. Like a sodality the confraternity has corporate structure. The basis of distinction is to be found in the specific purpose of each. While a sodality is founded for any religious purpose, a confraternity is established for the promotion of public worship.[33] The promotion of public worship may assume any one of a number of practical forms: the fostering of devotion to the Blessed Sacrament

---

fieri omnino debet; imo haec inscriptio, si associatio in personam moralem erecta fuerit, est ad validitatem necessaria."

[31]Canon 542, §2: "Ut autem de admissione constet, inscriptio in albo consociationis fieri omnino debet; haec inscriptio, si consociatio in personam moralem erecta fuerit et ad modum organici corporis constituta, est ad validitatem necessaria."—Motu Proprio *Cleri Sanctitati.*

[32]This opinion seems to be favored also by the carefully chosen phraseology of the response of the Commission for the Interpretation of the Code of Canon Law, March 6, 1927: "Utrum vi canonis 711, §2 locorum Ordinarii stricte teneantur *erigere* in qualibet parochia confraternitatem SS. Sacramenti, an ejus loco possint, secundum peculiaria adiuncta, *instituere* piam unionem vel sodalitatem SS. Sacramenti.—*Negative ad primam partem, affirmative ad secundam partem.—AAS,* XIX (1927), 161. The use of *erigere* in a formal legal context implies, if it does not definitely indicate, moral personality; whereas, *instituere* is disassociated from such legal implication. Canon 555 of the Oriental Code of Canon Law is equally circumspect in its choice of words.—Motu Proprio *Cleri Sanctitati.*

[33]Canons 707, §2 and 708. Cf. S. C. Ep. et Reg., *Romana,* 18 ian. 1907—*Fontes,* n. 2054, for the threefold distinction of confraternity in pre-Code legislation.

(e.g., the many confraternities of the Most Blessed Sacrament, the nocturnal adoration confraternities) or the promotion of special devotion to the Blessed Virgin Mary (e.g., the various confraternities of the Most Holy Rosary). For all that, it is essential for a confraternity to be engaged in and foster public devotion,[34] since the Code of Canon Law expressly insists on this requisite.[35]

A confraternity is always a moral person and must be constituted *ad modum organici corporis* according to the prescriptions of the Code of Canon Law. However, in the actual classification of ecclesiastical associations bearing the name of confraternity, some ancient ecclesiastical societies may not lend themselves to ready classification according to the categories described in the canons. The difficulty stems from the fact that many of these societies possess special privileges, while others, by reason of their antiquity, have attained a number of time-honored customs. Nevertheless, the proper definition of a confraternity, as formulated in the Code of Canon Law, contains three essential elements: first, it must be a moral person (canon 708); secondly, it must be a sodality, that is, set up *ad modum organici corporis* (canons 707, §1 and 707, §2); lastly, its specific purpose is the promotion of public worship (707, §2).[36]

Section 3: *Division of Primary Societies*

Another canonical division of ecclesiastical associations is based on the form of recognition given the association by the Holy See. Under this classification are included: primary unions, archsodalities and archconfraternities. Such primary associations usually enjoy the right to affiliate other associations and to communicate to their affiliates whatever privi-

[34]Public devotion is described in canon 1256 in these terms: "Cultus, si deferatur nomine Ecclesiae a personis legitime ad hoc deputatis et per actus ex Ecclesiae institutione Deo, Sanctis ac Beatis tantum exhibendos, dicitur *publicus;*..."

[35]Canon 707, §2: "Sodalitia vero in incrementum quoque publici cultus erecta, speciali nomine *confraternitates* appellantur."

[36]Cf. Cappello, F., *Summa Iuris Canonici* (5. ed., 3 vols., Roma: Universitas Gregoriana, 1951-1955), II, p. 119; Vromant, G.-Bongaerts, L., *De Fidelium Associationibus,* p. 100; Vermeersch, A.-Creusen, I., *Epitome Iuris Canonici* (7. ed., 3 vols., Parisiis: Desclée De Brouwer, 1946-1954), I, n. 855. Fanfani, L., *De Iure Religiosorum* (Rovigo: Istituto Padano di Arti Grafiche, 1949), n. 550, seems to hold that the only essential determinant of a confraternity is the purpose of promoting public worship.

leges they themselves possess. The notions of *affiliation* and *communication of privileges* will be treated in later chapters. It suffices here to note that primary associations regularly enjoy the faculty to affiliate and communicate privileges which the Holy See alone can grant to them. Sometimes the status of *primary society* is given merely by way of an honorary title, without the power to affiliate and communicate privileges being attached.[37] Even so, the conferral of this dignity is the exclusive right of the Holy See.[38]

Primary societies may be classified according to their particular internal organization either as a pious union, sodality or confraternity. A pious union which is raised to the dignity of a primary society is called a *primary union*. In view of its power to affiliate other pious unions with the same title and same purpose, the primary union may communicate its spiritual privileges and indulgences according to the norms of canon law.[39]

The second type of primary association is the *archsodality*. Constituted *ad modum organici corporis,* this sodality is an association which has received the primary status from the Holy See. It enjoys the privilege of communicating its spiritual privileges and indulgences to other similar societies. The distinction between an archsodality and a primary union stems from the fundamental difference between a sodality and a pious union, since the conferral of primary status does not affect the intrinsic nature of an ecclesiastical society.

An *archconfraternity* is a confraternity which has received the same

[37]Canon 725. Cf. *AAS,* I (1909), 759; IV (1912), 97.

[38]On occasion one encounters the words *primary congregations, primary societies* used interchangeably for the more specific term *primary union*. In this sense canon 720 uses *primary congregations,* and *primary societies* which are not otherwise expressly defined by the Code of Canon Law. Many documents use these terms indiscriminately, e.g. S. C. C., *Corrienten.,* 13 nov. 1920—*AAS,* XIII (1921), 141: "... quam pleraeque societates et confraternitates vere ecclesiasticae." The editor of the *Rescripta Authentica S. C. Indulg.* remarks: "Quam denominationes *Archiconfraternitatum, Archisodalitatum, Confraternitatum, Sodalitatum,* etc., in documentis huc pertinentibus et in ipsis Summariis indulgentiarum non sint omnino fixae et stabiles, sed saepe promiscue adhibeantur (confer ex. gr. Summarium n. 29, p. 457 ubi *Piae Unioni SS. Cordis Jesu* vix non omnes tribuuntur) ideo Summaria secundum eas denominationes accurate disponi non poterant." p. 707, nota (1). Cf. also *AAS,* IV (1912), 721.

[39]Cf. canons 720, 721, §2, 722. The essential elements in the definition will be examined in chapter IV of this dissertation.

title of dignity as the archsodality and primary union. If it receives the faculty to affiliate, the archconfraternity may, through affiliation, communicate to similar confraternities its own privileges and indulgences. The rank of archconfraternity, archsodality and primary union, it has been noted, may be granted to associations *honoris causa.*[40] However, such conferrals of an honorary nature are not the common practice of the Holy See. For when an ecclesiastical society is raised to the status of a primary society, the Holy See ordinarily grants it the power to affiliate and communicate its privileges.[41]

[40]Canon 725.—"Titulus *archisodalitii* vel *archiconfraternitatis* vel *unionis primariae,* etiam honoris tantum causa, potest associationi ab una Sede Apostolica concedi."

[41]Canon 720.—"Sodalitia quae iure pollent alias eiusdem speciei associationes sibi aggregandi, *archisodalitia,* vel *archiconfraternitates,* vel piae uniones, congregationes, societates *primariae* appellantur." Cf. Tachy, A., *Traité des Confréries* (Amiens: Jourdain-Rousseau, 1896), p. 137.

CHAPTER IV

ARCHCONFRATERNITIES, ARCHSODALITIES, PRIMARY UNIONS

Article 1: Definition and Division

Section 1: *Terminology*

In the pre-Code legislation the terminology used to designate archconfraternities and primary unions was lacking in desired clarity and consistency. The editor of the *Rescripta Authentica* of the Sacred Congregation of Indulgences underscores the indiscriminate use of the terms *archconfraternity* and *archsodality,* along with other designations for ecclesiastical societies, in documents and summaries of indulgences published by the Sacred Congregation.[1] After the Code of Canon Law a similar lack of consistency is evident in the use of terminology for ecclesiastical associations, so that terms like *archconfraternity* and *archsodality* are still used interchangeably in the official documents.[2] The Code of Canon Law itself is inconsistent in employing the term *primary union.* The title of chapter III reads: *De Archiconfraternitatibus et primariis unionibus,* omitting altogether the proper title of *archsodality.* Canon 724 speaks of the transfer of archconfraternities and primary unions and once again does not mention archsodality. It is evident in both these instances that the concept of *archsodality* is categorized under the broader term *primary union,* since the three types of affiliating associations are professedly treated in canon 720 and once again in canon 725.

The three titles, archconfraternity, archsodality and primary union, listed in canon 720, are the technical designations for the different types of affiliating societies. These three kinds of affiliating associations correspond to the three basic types of ecclesiastical associations: the con-

[1]*Rescripta Authentica S. C. Indulg.,* p. 707 footnote (1). Cf. *AAS,* IV (1912), 721 for an example of a document that uses the terms *archconfraternity* and *archsodality* interchangeably. S. C. Ep. et Reg., 12 ian. 1880—*ASS,* XII (1880), 587, uses the term *archassociation.*

[2]Cf. *AAS,* XIX (1927), 398.

fraternity, sodality and pious union.[3] It is worth noting that beside these specific terms, *archconfraternity, archsodality,* and *primary union,* canon 720 adds *primary congregations* and *societies.*[4] These last two designations were widely used in the pre-Code period as general terms to denote various primary unions. In the canons dealing with ecclesiastical associations the terms *congregation* and *society* occur without technical definitions, so that they may be employed as generic terms equivalent to the concept of ecclesiastical *association.*[5] Because of this fluctuation in terminology it is not unusual in papal documents to find the terms *archconfraternity* and *archsodality* applied to an association which is, in reality, a primary union. Often, too, one finds the phrase *primary congregation* or *primary society* used to designate what is actually an archsodality.[6] For this reason then, the terms selected to refer to particular associations in papal documents represent on the whole tenuous evidence as to the specific nature of the association in question.[7]

For the sake of clarity, the terms *archconfraternity, archsodality* and *primary union* will be used in their technical meanings throughout the canonical section of this dissertation. By the same token, the expressions *primary associations* and *primary societies* will be employed as generic designations to include all three types. When reference is made to a particular association, the official title, as found in papal documents, will be used.

[3]Canon 707.

[4]Canon 720: Sodalitia quae iure pollent alias eiusdem speciei associationes sibi aggregandi, *archisodalitia,* vel *archiconfraternitates,* vel piae uniones, congregationes, societates *primariae* appellantur.

[5]Cf. Pius XII, const. apost. "*Bis Saeculari,*" 27 sept. 1948—*AAS,* XL (1948), 393 ff. This document employs interchangeably the designations *sodalitium, societas, consociatio, congregatio.* Cf. also Pius XII, epist. "*De Congregationibus Marianis provehendis,*" 15 apr. 1950—*AAS,* XLII (1950), 437 ff.

[6]Cf. *AAS,* IV (1912), 721; XIX (1927), 249, 398.

[7]The Latin Code of Canon Law (canon 711, §2) and many papal documents speak of the *confraternity* of Christian Doctrine. However, the Oriental Code of Canon Law (Motu Proprio *Cleri Sanctitati,* canon 555) speaks of the *sodalitium* of Christian Doctrine, as does also the Sacred Congregation of the Council in its decree of Jan. 12, 1935—*AAS,* XXVII (1935), 149. From a technical standpoint, a confraternity, in addition to other constitutive elements, must have for its purpose the furthering of public cult. In a proper sense, therefore, ecclesiastical associations of Christian Doctrine are not confraternities, but sodalities. Cf. canon 707.

Section 2: *Definition of Primary Societies*

Canon 720 and canon 722, §1 conjointly present a definition of primary societies. Both juridical units identify primary societies as associations which enjoy the power to affiliate to themselves similar associations in order to communicate indulgences, privileges and spiritual favors.[8] The communication of privileges is a direct result of affiliation and will be treated at length in chapter V. The present section is concerned exclusively with the concept of affiliation and the various types of affiliating societies.

The notion of affiliation involves an authoritative act by which one association is joined to another. The resultant unity is of a moral character and is externally signified by the relationship which arises from the jurisdictional act of the proper authority in the affiliating association. As a direct result of the bond of affiliation, the communication of certain privileges and indulgences from the primary society to its affiliates is effected.[9] Although, as a general rule, archconfraternities and primary unions enjoyed the power to affiliate, the simple title of archconfraternity or primary union was, in the pre-Code period, conferred from time to time upon a number of associations merely for honorary reasons. Under such circumstances the faculty of affiliation was obviously absent. For instance, St. Pius X elevated a confraternity of the Immaculate Conception to the rank of archconfraternity, but the title was a simple honorary concession.[10] The Code of Canon Law itself explicitly provides for the bestowal of the title of primary status for purely honorary reasons.[11] Hence, the mere conferral of a primary title upon an ecclesiastical association does not *ipso facto* impart the power to affiliate. The granting of the faculty to affiliate other associations is always expressly referred to in the apostolic indult which raises a society to a primary one.[12] Conversely, whenever express mention of this power is not made,

[8]Canon 720 uses the verb *aggregare* which this dissertation will render "affiliate" throughout.

[9]Cf. Barbier de Montault, X. "Affiliation de la cathédrale de Nevers à la basilique patriarcale de Latran," *Analecta Iuris Pontificii,* XII (1873), p. 923.

[10]Pius X, 31 iul. 1909—*AAS,* I (1909), 759. For other examples confer Paul III, 7 febr. 1541—*Bull. Rom. Taur.,* VI, p. 306; Pius X, 29 ian. 1912—*AAS,* IV (1912), 97.

[11]Canon 725.

[12]Cf. *Rescripta Authentica S. C. Indulg.,* p. 703: "Aggregandi facultatem non

the indult invariably indicates that the title of archconfraternity or primary union is being conferred merely *honoris causa.*[13]

Section 3: *Division of Primary Societies*

The fundamental division of ecclesiastical societies into confraternities, sodalities and pious unions,[14] provides the basis for the threefold division of primary associations into archconfraternities, archsodalities and primary unions.[15] Since the fundamental notions and distinctive traits of these three subgroups of ecclesiastical societies have already been discussed in chapter III, it remains only to apply them to the concept of primary society.

Juridically, an archconfraternity is a confraternity which possesses the power to affiliate other confraternities of the same kind. The precise meaning of this phrase "of the same kind" has reference both to the title and purpose of the society seeking affiliation. Not only the official designation of the association but also the purpose for which it is constituted are, therefore, of primary significance.[16] Thus, for example, an archconfraternity of the Immaculate Heart of Mary can only affiliate confraternities with the same official title and oriented towards the same specific purpose. This does not mean that an affiliate must adopt or employ the same statutes as its primary society, but it does mean that

---

habent confraternitates quaelibet ipsa sua erectione sed solum ex concessione S. Sedis." For an example of a pre-Code formulary granting an association the title of primary union and the faculty to affiliate confer the appendix. For an example of an indult granted after the Code of Canon Law, cf. *AAS*, XLVI (1954), 363.

13 For an example of such a bestowal, cf. *AAS*, I (1909), 759. For the refusal of a petition from an association aspiring to the rank of archconfraternity, confer the decree of the Sacred Congregation of Indulgences, 31 aug. 1722—*Rescripta Authentica S. C. Indulg.*, n. 43.

14 Canon 707.

15 Canon 720.

16 Canon 721, §2. The individual elements that must be identical in the primary society and its affiliates will be given extended treatment in the following chapter when the conditions for affiliation will be examined. It should be noted here, however, that the phrase of canon 720 *eiusdem speciei* must be interpreted in the light of pre-Code legislation and in conjunction with canon 721, §2 which embodies a different expression, namely, *eiusdem tituli ac finis.*

both must pursue the same specific objective for which the primary society has been established.[17]

Now it follows that the archconfraternity must itself possess the elements essential to the confraternity; namely, moral personality, corporate internal organization, and the explicit purpose of promoting public worship. When a confraternity has received the dignity of archconfraternity, its nature is not changed. The archconfraternity retains its original juridic structure and distinguishing properties. For this reason the distinction between a confraternity and an archconfraternity is one of rank rather than of nature, of degree rather than of kind. An archconfraternity, even without the faculty of affiliation, enjoys a distinction of dignity because of its honorary title. As such, it is equal to another archconfraternity which possesses the power to affiliate. Accordingly, in a true and proper sense, archconfraternities are of equal grade and degree whether they have the faculty of affiliation or not.[18]

The same conclusion holds true in the case of the other two types of primary societies, the archsodality, and the primary union. If the dignity of archsodality is conferred upon a sodality, its internal nature and juridic status remain essentially the same. The newly bestowed dignity of archsodality merely adds an extrinsic difference in rank.[19] Similarly, pious unions which have been raised to the grade of primary unions retain their juridic structure and intrinsic nature. No substantial change is effected by the conferral of primary status to an ecclesiastical society.[20]

In listing the divisions of associations which enjoy the faculty to affiliate, the Code of Canon Law (canon 720) mentions *primary congregations* and *primary societies*. These expressions do not provide the basis for further divisions among affiliating societies. They are, in fact,

[17]Cf. *S. C. Indulg., Lemovicen.*, 22 aug. 1842—*Fontes*, n. 5027.

[18]Discussion of the dignity of archconfraternities and primary unions is reserved for chapter VI dealing with precedence (cf. p. 95 ff. below).

[19]The Code of Canon Law insists on the accidental difference between a sodality and an archsodality between a confraternity and an archconfraternity, between a primary union and a pious union (cf. canon 701).

[20]Canon 720.—"Sodalitia quae iure pollent alias ejusdem speciei associationes sibi aggregandi, *archisodalitia*, vel *archiconfraternitates*, vel piae uniones, congregationes, societates *primariae* appellantur." The first word of this canon, *sodalitia*, is not used in its technical meaning (canon 707, §1) and is to be taken rather, on the basis of textual considerations, in the generic sense of association.

generic terms used on occasion to denote primary unions, archsodalities and even archconfraternities.[21]

Article 2: Constitution, Transfer, and Suppression of Primary Societies

The Holy See has the exclusive right to raise an association to the status of primary society.[22] Even before the Code of Canon Law the concession of the title of archconfraternity or primary union was reserved to the Holy See. From earliest times, in fact, the Holy Father granted this title as a pontifical honor to associations outstanding for spiritual influence or apostolic effectiveness.[23] Since the title of primary society entailed a certain right of precedence over other societies, the Holy See never delegated the power to create primary societies. Another reason for the Roman Pontiffs' unwavering policy of reservation centered around the fact that the Holy See granted to the newly elevated primary society the faculty to affiliate. This power to affiliate always involved a communication of privileges and indulgences already granted or to be granted in the future to the primary society. By its nature the communication of indulgences and privileges implies a reduplication of the original grant each time a new association is affiliated. Indeed, each affiliation effects a concession of the privileges and indulgences enjoyed by the primary association. Consequently, the Holy See never delegated its power of raising associations to the status of primary associations—it always reserved this right to itself, to the exclusion of all others.[24]

Periodically the Sovereign Pontiffs have used Apostolic Letters to grant the title of primary status to a society.[25] In other instances they

[21]Cf. Vromant, G.-Bongaerts, L., *De Fidelium Associationibus*, p. 117, who rightly consider the Marian Congregations to be confraternities. The *Prima Primaria* Congregation of the Roman College is actually an archconfraternity possessing the power to affiliate, as is evident from the "*Bis Saeculari*," of Pius XII, 27 sept. 1948—*AAS*, XL (1948), 393.

[22]Canons 721, §1 and 725.

[23]Cf. Secret. Brevium, litt. 5 iul. 1881—*Fontes*, n. 6458.

[24]Conc. Trident., sess. XXV, *decret. de indulg.;* S. C. Indulg., *Quiten.*, 12 ian. 1878—*Fontes*, n. 5081.

[25]Cf. *Analecta Iuris Pontificii*, IX (1867), 1024; *AAS*, XLVI (1954), 363.

have granted this dignity through the Sacred Congregation of Indulgences.[26] For mission areas the Sacred Congregation for the Propagation of the Faith has enjoyed competence in this matter.[27]

Since the promulgation of the Code of Canon Law, the Sacred Congregation of the Council has competence over associations of the faithful.[28] Applications requesting this dignity in behalf of an association should be sent to this Congregation. However, the request should be addressed directly to the Holy Father, after having been drawn up by the local Ordinary in whose diocese the association is situated. If the society is under the jurisdiction of a religious institute, the major superior[29] of the religious institute should formulate the petition, and an accompanying letter of recommendation from the local Ordinary is to be included. An example of a formulary that may be used is found on page 73. In mission territories the application should be directed to the Sacred Congregation for the Propagation of the Faith.

The petition or the accompanying letter of recommendation serves the purpose of outlining the reasons for granting the request. In the past the Roman Pontiffs bestowed the rank of primary association and the privilege to affiliate, in consideration of the rapidity of growth attained by a certain type of association in a given region. Other confraternities were granted the status of an archconfraternity by reason of their antiquity or even the impressive number of its members. Still other associations, for the most part in mission countries, were accorded this honor with a view to encouraging a certain type of spiritual activity or a special form of Christian piety.[30]

The right to transfer a primary society from one place to another is reserved to the Holy See.[31] Just as the Holy See limits to itself the power to create archconfraternities and primary unions, so too it reserves the power to transfer them from one place to another. In ex-

[26] S. C. Indulg., 1 febr. 1879—*ASS*, XI (1878-1879), 608.

[27] Consult the appendix for the document constituting the *Archconfraternity of Christian Mothers* in St. Augustine's Church, Pittsburgh, Pa.

[28] Canon 250, §2.

[29] By major superior is understood the Provincial Superior under whose jurisdiction the society is situated. Cf. Vromant G.-Bongaerts, L., *De Fidelium Associationibus*, pp. 26-27.

[30] Cf. Tachy, A., *Traité des Confréries*, pp. 139-145.

[31] Canon 724.

pressing this juridic restriction, canon 724 uses the generic term *sedes*.[32] Insofar as a primary association may be established in conjunction with a church, oratory, or semi-public oratory,[33] the Code of Canon Law employs terminology susceptible of the broadest interpretation to proscribe any transferral from the place where an association was situated at the time of its elevation to a primary society.

The Code of Canon Law does not speak of the suppression of a primary society as such. Canon 699, §2, however, lays down the general principle that only the Holy See can suppress an association which it has established.[34] Since the creation and transferral of primary societies are reserved exclusively to the Holy See, it follows that the Holy See alone possesses the power to suppress them.[35]

Article 3: The Power to Affiliate

Section 1: *Religious Institutes*

The power to affiliate associations and to communicate apostolic privileges and indulgences is distinct from the power to establish associations. The former inheres solely in the supreme authority of the Roman Pontiff,[36] while the latter is an integral element of the jurisdiction of the local Ordinary. This distinction is fundamental, and, if not kept in proper perspective, leads to confused notions concerning the exercise of these separate powers.

In the course of history, the Roman Pontiffs have granted to some religious institutes not only the faculty to establish certain associations, but also the privilege to affiliate these same organizations to a primary society canonically established in one of their churches. For example, the Father General of the Society of Jesus has the exclusive power to establish the Sodality of Our Lady in places belonging to or under the

[32]Canon 724.—"Archiconfraternitas vel primaria unio de alia ad aliam sedem nonnisi ab Apostolica Sede transferri potest."

[33]Canon 712, §1. Cf. Seraphinus de Angelis, *De Fidelium Associationibus*, I, p. 56.

[34]Canon 699, §2. "Associationes vero ab ipsa Apostolica Sede erectae nonnisi ab eadem supprimi possunt."

[35]Cf. *ASS*, XI (1878-1879), 608.

[36]Denziger, H.-Bannwart, C.-Umberg, J., *Enchiridion Symbolorum, Definitionum, et Declarationum de Rebus Fidei et Morum* (26. ed., Friburgi Brisgoviae: Herder, 1947,) n. 757.

jurisdiction of the Jesuits. In all other places, the sodality may be established either by the local Ordinary on his own authority, or by the Father General with the consent of the local Ordinary. On the other hand, the Father General of the Society of Jesus alone has the power to affiliate sodalities to the Archsodality of the Roman College—the *conditio sine qua non* for the communication of spiritual privileges and indulgences. This power he enjoys to the exclusion of all others.[37] In his case, both powers inhere in one and the same person, but each is the subject of a separate and distinct act.[38]

These considerations notwithstanding, certain religious institutes have received the power both to establish and to affiliate associations by virtue of one and the same formal act. For example, the Father General of the Order of Preachers has been granted the twofold, simultaneous power to establish and to affiliate Confraternities of the Most Holy Rosary. In his case, the automatic affiliation and communication of privileges and indulgences are effected in and through the very act of establishing the confraternity. Thus, two distinct yet simultaneous effects derive from the one formal act.[39]

Section 2: *Primary Societies*

The power to establish associations similar to themselves is not conferred upon archconfraternities and primary unions. In point of fact, this power has never been granted to them by the Holy See, since its unlimited exercise would prejudice the unity of authority in the individual diocese. Under ordinary circumstances, the local Ordinary is best qualified to pass judgment on the usefulness of various types of associations in his territory. It is his responsibility to govern the diocese, to oversee its organized activities, and to give meaning and motive to the piety of his subjects so that the Catholic faith may flourish among

[37]Pius XII, const. apost. *"Bis Saeculari,"* 27 sept. 1948—*AAS,* XL (1948), 393.

[38]The Father General of the Redemptorists has similar powers with regard to the Association of Our Lady of Perpetual Help. Cf. Seeberger, M., *Key to the Spiritual Treasures,* p. 166.

[39]Cf. Leo XIII, const. apost. *"Ubi primum,"* 2 oct. 1898—*ASS,* XXXI (1898-1899), 257 ff. For a discussion of the faculty of affiliation enjoyed by Ordinaries in missions consult Vromant, G.-Bongaerts, L., *De Fidelium Associationibus,* pp. 31-32.

the people committed to his care.[40] This fact fundamentally accounts for the policy of the Roman Pontiffs in their insistence that ecclesiastical associations be directly subject to them. Even in the case of associations reserved to religious, the Holy See nearly always requires the consent of the local Ordinary for their establishment.[41]

Although archconfraternities and primary unions never receive the faculty to establish associations, they do receive the power to affiliate other associations. The Roman Pontiffs have been generous in raising associations to the status of archconfraternities and primary unions and in granting them the power to communicate privileges and indulgences through such affiliation. Since the act of affiliation consists primarily in the transmission of indulgences and spiritual favors from the primary society to its affiliate, there is little likelihood that the granting of such power will disturb or disrupt the singleness of authority within a diocese. The primary society does not acquire authority over its affiliates. As a result, conflicts over the immediate subjection of an association to the local Ordinary are virtually excluded. Moreover, by way of precautionary measure, one of the conditions for the valid affiliation of an association to a primary society is the written consent and recommendation of the local Ordinary.[42]

The precise extent of the faculty to affiliate is determined by the terms of the grant as expressed in the apostolic indult. Actual cases reveal two distinct types of faculties. The first type of indult empowers the primary society to affiliate similar societies all over the world. The second type restricts the faculty to affiliate to a particular territory or region. Archconfraternities and primary unions established in Rome usually enjoy the privilege to affiliate both within that city and throughout the world.[43] Those associations outside of Rome that have been raised to the dignity of primary society ordinarily receive a limited faculty of affiliation.[44] Nevertheless, the Holy See has at times granted

[40]Canons 335 and 336.

[41]Canon 686.

[42]Canon 723.

[43]Documents which grant the unlimited faculty to affiliate usually employ expressions such as *ubique terrarum, ubivis locorum.* In all cases of restricted faculties, the limits set to the concession are expressly defined. Cf. Seraphinus de Angelis, *De Fidelium Associationibus,* p. 67.

[44]Secret. Brevium, litt. 5 iul. 1881—*Fontes,* n. 6458: "Ove non si tratti di Con-

to primary societies established outside of Rome the faculty to affiliate similar associations all over the world.[45]

Canon 721, §2 lays down the general norm for affiliation: primary societies can only affiliate societies which have the same title and purpose, unless the apostolic indult states otherwise. The phrase *eiusdem tituli ac finis,* used in the canon, does not differ in meaning from the phrases *eiusdem tituli et instituti,* and *eiusdem denominationis et instituti.* All these expressions are found in documents creating primary societies,[46] and help to explain the terminology of canon 720 which empowers primary societies to affiliate associations of the same kind (*eiusdem speciei*).

When canon 700 speaks of three types (*species*) of ecclesiastical associations, namely, third orders secular, confraternities, and pious unions, it employs the term at issue to denote three generic divisions. On the other hand, canon 720 uses this term with respect to organizations which are subdivisions of these three main categories. Thus the word *species* has a much broader meaning in canon 700 than it has in canon 720. In effect, the division of ecclesiastical associations into third orders secular, confraternities and pious unions represents a listing of the various classes of associations, and therefore sets down the broadest division possible. Canon 720 contemplates a twofold division within a different frame of reference; namely, confraternities and pious unions, and classifies sodalities under the latter.[47] The term *species* of canon 720, then, does not have direct reference to these divisions, rather it has a much more limited meaning. In fact, the entire chapter of the Code of Canon Law in which canon 720 is found,[48] places limits and conditions upon the concept of affiliation which explain the full import of the phrase

---

fraternite erette in insigni Santuari, non suole concedersi il titolo di Arciconfraternita colla facoltà di aggregare fuori della diocesi; o della provincia ecclesiastica se il Sodalizio si trova istituito nella diocesi del Metropolitano."

45Cf. Pius X, litt. apost. *"Plane compertum,"* 21 maii 1912—*AAS,* IV (1912), 439.

46S. C. Indulg., *Albien.,* 17 iul. 1891—*Fontes,* n. 5112; S. C. Indulg., 19 maii 1733—*Rescripta Authentica S. C. Indulg.,* n. 92; S. R. Rota, *Militen.,* 25 ian. 1913—*AAS,* V (1913), 74 ff.

47Cf. Lib. II, Pars III, Caput II. The canons throughout presuppose two classes of ecclesiastical associations: confraternities on the one hand, and pious unions on the other. This second category includes sodalities.

48Lib. II, Pars III, Caput III.

eiusdem speciei. Only in the second paragraph of canon 721 does the Code of Canon Law give the essential meaning of the phrase when it asserts that primary societies can only affiliate societies with the same title and purpose.[49]

In view of the foregoing, associations of the same kind (*eiusdem speciei*) are those which have the same title and purpose. That is, for affiliation purposes, they must share a common title and objective with the affiliating primary society.[50] The title refers to the official name which properly designates the association. This includes not only a general identification of the society but also the specific name. For instance, the Sacred Congregation of Indulgences insisted that a primary *Bona Mors* society whose official title was "Associatio Bonae Mortis D. N. Jesu Christi morientis ac Beatissimae Virginis Mariae ejus Genetricis perdolentis" could not grant affiliation to an association with the title "Bonae Mortis Sancti Josephi."[51]

Identity of purpose must be interpreted in terms of the specific aim and objective of the association. Confraternities of the Most Holy Rosary and of the Scapular of Mount Carmel have the same generic purpose of promoting honor to the Blessed Virgin Mary, but while one achieves its objective through the recitation of the rosary, the other pursues its purpose through the wearing of the scapular. An archconfraternity of the Scapular of Mount Carmel, it follows, may not affiliate a confraternity of the Most Holy Rosary.[52]

Identity of title and purpose is, therefore, a condition for valid affiliation. This can be inferred from the text of canon 721, whose first paragraph expressly requires an apostolic indult for the valid affiliation of associations. In the second paragraph, the legislator requires an express grant of power within the indult for the affiliation of associations of diverse title and purpose. Accordingly, if the express faculty to affiliate associations of diverse title and purpose is not given, the primary society clearly lacks the required power and any attempt at affiliation is invalid. Besides, canon 721 makes reference to legislation prior to the

[49]Canon 721, §2. "Archiconfraternitas vel primaria unio eas tantum potest confraternitates vel pias uniones sibi aggregare, quae sint eiusdem tituli ac finis, nisi indultum apostolicum aliud ferat."

[50]Canon 721, §2.

[51]S. C. Indulg., *Albien.*, 17 iul. 1891—*Fontes*, n. 5112.

[52]Cf. S. C. Indulg., *Papien.*, 20 iul. 1728—*Fontes*, n. 4964.

Code of Canon Law which prevented, under pain of nullity, all attempts at affiliating associations of diverse title or purpose,[53] and this, in virtue of the fact that the grant of power from the Roman Pontiff was restricted to the affiliation of like associations.[54] Consequently, any act in contravention to the nature of the indult or proceeding beyond its express grant of power was *ipso facto* null and void.

Nevertheless, there have been instances when the Roman Pontiffs consigned to primary societies the power to affiliate diverse associations. The archconfraternity of the Assumption established in the Church of Santa Maria in Monterone at Rome possesses such a faculty. This archconfraternity can affiliate associations of diverse title and purpose on the proviso that the affiliate adds to its official title, *ad levamen animarum in purgatorio existentium.*[55] Admittedly, such a grant of power is extremely rare.[56]

Identity of title and purpose as a condition for affiliating associations neither signifies nor implies identity of statutes. As long as the association to be affiliated has the same specific end, the means to that end may or may not be identical. The statutes, the manner of implementing the charitable works proper to the association, the prescribed prayers, the habit worn by the members need not reveal on the part of the affiliates either convergence upon or conformity to the primary society.[57] Needless to add, if a certain prayer or work is enjoined for the gaining of an indulgence communicated by affiliation, such a prayer or work always remains an indispensable condition for the indulgence. But the point at issue here refers only to the works and prayers peculiar to the primary society. None of these are in any way incumbent

[53]*Ibidem.*

[54]Cf. Tachy, A., *Traité des Confréries,* p. 153; Beringer, F.-Steinen, P., *Die Ablaesse,* II, n. 122; Amanieu, A., "Archiconfrérie," *DDC,* col. 942; Seraphinus de Angelis, *De Fidelium Associationibus,* I, p. 67; Vromant, G.-Bongaerts, L., *De Fidelium Associationibus,* p. 121.

[55]S. C. Indulg., 23 aug. 1861—*Rescripta Authentica S. C. Indulg.,* n. 402.

[56]Cf. Tachy, A., *Traité des Confréries,* p. 152.

[57]S. C. Indulg., *Utinen.,* 9 dec. 1862—*ASS,* II (1866), 534; S. C. Indulg., 20 mart. 1747—*Decreta Authentica Sacrae Congregationis Indulgentiis sacrisque Reliquiis praepositae ab anno* 1668 *ad annum* 1882 *edita iussu et auctoritate Leonis XIII* (Ratisbonae, 1883), n. 163 (hereafter cited: *Decreta Authentica S. C. Indulg.*).

upon the affiliate nor is the affiliate in any way subject to the primary association.[58]

With regard to confraternities of the Blessed Sacrament and sodalities of Christian Doctrine, the formalities of affiliation are subject to special legislation. By common law the affiliation of confraternities of the Most Blessed Sacrament and sodalities of Christian Doctrine to their respective primary societies in Rome takes place as soon as they are established. This immediacy of affiliation derives from the operation of the law, independently of a special jurisdictional act. Once the confraternity is legitimately established, the affiliation takes place *ipso iure*. Concerning the affiliation of associations of the Blessed Sacrament, the Pontifical Commission for the interpretation of the Code of Canon Law has declared that *sodalities* and *pious unions* of the Blessed Sacrament are not *ipso iure* affiliated to the Archconfraternity of the Blessed Sacrament in the Church of *Santa Maria sopra Minerva* in Rome.[59] The Commission neither rules out nor discourages the sending of a regular petition for affiliation to the Archconfraternity in Rome by a pious union of the Most Blessed Sacrament. The decree simply states that affiliation in the case under discussion is not effected *ipso iure*. Legitimately established associations of the Most Blessed Sacrament seeking affiliation should, therefore, apply directly to the Archconfraternity in Rome.[60]

A proper evaluation of this reply of the Commission for the Interpretation of the Code of Canon Law requires an analysis of the text of canon 711, §2. The canon, according to the reply of the Commission, merely provides for the automatic affiliation of confraternities of the Most Blessed Sacrament. Confraternities must be understood in the strict sense of canon 707, §2, namely, societies possessing corporate organization and moral personality, in addition to the particular purpose of promoting public worship. Confraternities, then, which promote the public worship of the Blessed Sacrament are affiliated *ipso iure* to the Archconfraternity established in Rome.

It must be recalled that any society of the Most Blessed Sacrament other than a confraternity must fulfill all the conditions stipulated by law if it is to become affiliated with the Archconfraternity in Rome. For

[58]Canon 722, §2.

[59]PCI, 6 mart. 1927, ad II—*AAS*, XIX (1927), 161.

[60]Cf. Vermeersch, A., *Periodica*, XVI (1927), p. 58; Regatillo E., *Interpretatio et Iurisprudentia Codicis Iuris Canonici* (3. ed., Santander: Sal Terrae, 1953), p. 274.

affiliation, therefore, an association of the Most Blessed Sacrament must have the same title and specific purpose (promotion of public worship of the Blessed Sacrament) as the affiliating archconfraternity, and have according to the interpretation of most authors, juridic personality.[61] These three elements according to the common opinion are inalterably demanded of every association requesting affiliation. In applying these prescriptions to associations of the Blessed Sacrament which are not confraternities, one must keep in mind the basic definitions of confraternity, sodality, and pious union as set forth in canon 707. A sodality is an association which is constituted *ad modum organici corporis*. Thus, a sodality of the Most Blessed Sacrament would be an association constituted *ad modum organici corporis*, having for its purpose the increase of public worship of the Holy Eucharist.[62] Were such a sodality to seek affiliation, it would require according to the common opinion moral personality, in addition to the same title and purpose. But a sodality of the Blessed Sacrament which also has moral personality is by the very definition of the Code of Canon Law a confraternity,[63] and becomes *ipso iure* affiliated to the Archconfraternity in Rome.

Through a consistent application of the opinion which requires moral personality in an association to be affiliated, a different case obtains with pious unions of the Most Blessed Sacrament. A pious union is not constituted *ad modum organici corporis*. It may, however, be established as a moral person.[64] Thus, if a pious union of the Most Blessed Sacrament seeks affiliation with an archconfraternity, it must not only have the same title and specific purpose as the archconfraternity but it must also have juridic personality. Only when it has these essential properties, may it be affiliated through the formal act of the proper authority of the archconfraternity.[65]

A different interpretation of the reply of the Commission is given by those authors who hold that moral personality is not an essential requi-

[61]Cf. p. 64 ff. for an examination of the opinions concerning the necessity of moral personality in an association to be affiliated to a primary society.

[62]Cf. canon 555 of the Oriental Code of Canon Law (Motu Proprio *Cleri Sanctitati*).

[63]Canon 707, §2.

[64]Canon 708. Cf. p. 38 ff.

[65]Cf. page 65 ff.

site for valid affiliation.[66] According to this opinion the Commission for the Interpretation of the Code of Canon Law rules out the affiliation *ipso iure* of associations of the Most Blessed Sacrament which lack moral personality but does not deny that these same associations, as long as they have ecclesiastical approbation, may be affiliated through a formal act of the proper authority of the archconfraternity. In view of this opinion an association of the Most Blessed Sacrament, which has received the requisite ecclesiastical approval,[67] can be validly affiliated to the Archconfraternity of the Most Blessed Sacrament through a formal act of the competent authority of the Archconfraternity.[68]

The affiliation of associations of Christian Doctrine is likewise effected *ipso iure* once the requirements of law are satisfied. True, canon 711, §2 speaks of the confraternity of Christian Doctrine in this connection. However, the association of Christian Doctrine is not properly speaking a confraternity, since it does not have for its purpose the promotion of public worship but rather the systematic imparting of Christian doctrine.[69] It follows that it may be properly considered a pious union. Were it constituted *ad modum organici corporis,* it would become a sodality. For an association of Christian Doctrine to be affiliated *ipso iure* to the Archsodality of Christian Doctrine established in the Church of *Santa Maria del Pianto* in Rome, it must retain the specific title and purpose of the archsodality, over and above the qualification of canonical establishment.[70] A sodality or pious union of Christian Doctrine which fulfills these conditions achieves affiliation as soon as it is juridically established. Should an association of Christian Doctrine lack canonical establishment, or have a title or purpose different from the archsodality,

[66]Vermeersch, A., *Periodica,* XVI (1927), p. 58, along with others advances the opinion that moral personality is not a necessary condition for affiliation. For the examination and evaluation of the arguments in favor of this opinion consult p. 64 ff. of this dissertation.

[67]Cf. p. 36 ff.

[68]Cf. Vermeersch, A., *Periodica,* XVI (1927), p. 58.

[69]Cf. canon 555 of the Oriental Code of Canon Law (Motu Proprio *Cleri Sanctitati*) where the confraternity of the Most Blessed Sacrament and the sodality of Christian Doctrine are discussed in technical terms. The Sacred Congregation of the Council in its decree *Provido sane consilio,* Jan. 12, 1935, also makes the necessary distinction between the *confraternity* of the Most Blessed Sacrament and the *sodality* of Christian Doctrine—*AAS,* XXVII (1935), 145.

[70]Canon 711, §2. Cf. *AAS,* XXXII (1940), 58-59.

affiliation in virtue of canon 711, §2 or by formal act of affiliation on the part of the archsodality is impossible. The requirements for affiliation prescribed by the Code of Canon Law are exactly the same in both cases. Consequently, in the absence of an essential element for affiliation, affiliation by a formal act on the part of the society is ruled out on the same grounds.[71]

Only confraternities of the Most Blessed Sacrament and canonically instituted associations of Christian Doctrine are capable of affiliation in virtue of the operation of the law itself. In all other cases a formal act on the part of the primary society is needed. Manifestly, the act of affiliation remains distinct from the act of establishment.[72]

Section 3: *Exercise of the Power to Affiliate*

Primary societies which have the faculty to affiliate must exercise it through their supreme moderator or director. The text of the indult granting the power will ordinarily use the phrase ***supreme moderator*** or ***supreme director***. In each instance, the Holy See will unequivocally designate the head of the primary association who is to exercise the faculty and issue the diploma of affiliation.[73] If the faculty to affiliate is granted to a religious institute, the apostolic indult always mentions

[71]With regard to the affiliation of associations of Christian Doctrine there is the same division of opinion concerning their canonical establishment. Those authors who require moral personality of the association to be affiliated would demand that an association of Christian Doctrine be established as a moral person before an affiliation could be effected validly either *ipso iure* (canon 711, §2), or through a formal act of the Archsodality of Christian Doctrine. On the other hand, those canonists who hold that moral personality in the affiliate is not necessary require only ecclesiastical approbation of the association to be affiliated. Consult page 64 ff. for a fuller discussion of these opinions.

[72]The Major Basilicas in Rome also have the faculty to affiliate churches, chapels, etc., and even confraternities under special conditions. Cf. *Analecta Iuris Pontificii*, XII (1873), 826, 926. Benedict XIV, const. apost. "*Assiduae*," 2 iun. 1751—*Magnum Bullarium Romanum a beato Leone usque ad S. D. N. Benedictum XIV, seu Eiusdem Continuatio* (19 vols., Luxemburgi sumptibus Henrici-Alberti Gosse et Socii, 1727-1758), XVIII, 208. Cf. also *Decreta Authentica S. C. Indulg.*, nn. 25, 95.

[73]The formulary of affiliation prescribed in the decree of the Sacred Congregation of Indulgences, Jan. 8, 1861, employed the terms *Protector, Prior, Custos*. Any of these designations may be used in the apostolic indult to designate the head of the archconfraternity or primary union.—*Fontes*, n. 5074. Cf. canon 698.

the Superior General of the entire institute, to whom alone is imparted the right to exercise the faculty to affiliate. The Superior General of the Congregation of the Holy Redeemer, for example, has the exclusive power to affiliate associations of Our Lady of Perpetual Help.[74]

However, a question may arise concerning the delegation of this power of affiliation. Can the supreme moderator of an archconfraternity or primary union delegate this power to others, or must he without exception exercise it personally? Before the Code of Canon Law, supreme moderators could not delegate this power unless the power of delegation was expressly mentioned in the indult. On March 20, 1871, Pius IX validated all the affiliations of an archconfraternity in Paris attempted by subpromoters who had supposedly received delegated power from the supreme moderator of the archconfraternity. The Holy Father permitted the supreme moderator to make future affiliations but enjoined compliance with the constitution of Clement VIII (*Quaecumque*) and the decrees of the Sacred Congregation of Indulgences.[75]

On Dec. 13, 1892, the Sacred Congregation of Indulgences was asked whether the moderator of an archconfraternity or the Superior General of a religious institute with the faculty to affiliate might affix his name and official seal to a blank diploma of affiliation, which, being deposited at the diocesan chancery or in the house of a religious institute, might be filled out whenever an association applied for affiliation. The Sacred Congregation declared such an affiliation to be invalid.[76] The reason for the nullity of such affiliations arises from the fact that the supreme moderators of primary societies and Superiors General of affiliating religious institutes may not delegate their power of affiliation.[77]

Authors dealing with this question after the Code of Canon Law insist that the power to affiliate cannot be delegated, unless express mention of this fact is made in the apostolic indult. Seraphinus de Angelis explains that the faculty to affiliate is to be considered a privilege *praeter ius* and incommunicable since it inheres in the person of the supreme moderator or Superior General. This privilege cannot be

[74]Cf. Beringer, F.-Steinen, P., *Die Ablaesse*, II, n. 55.

[75]This document is reported in Beringer, F.-Steinen, P., *Die Ablaesse*, II, n. 127.

[76]S. C. Indulg., *Engolismen.*, 3 dec. 1892—*Fontes*, n. 5116.

[77]Tachy, A., *Traité des Confréries*, p. 138; Beringer, F.-Steinen, P., *Die Ablaesse*, II, n. 127; Amanieu, A., "Archiconfrérie," *DDC*, col. 935.

separated from his person unless the indult makes special provision to that effect.[78]

However, it may not be argued that this faculty is personal in that it resides in the supreme moderator or Religious Superior General. The power to affiliate is conferred upon the archconfraternity or primary union and inheres in the supreme office of these associations. In the case of the Religious Superiors General who are granted this power, the faculty is directly attached to their office and not communicated to them personally. Were a personal privilege at issue in such cases, the faculty would cease *ipso facto* when the term of office for the particular incumbent expires. Such is patently not the case. As a matter of fact, the power is granted to and inheres in the primary society as its personal privilege,[79] and the supreme moderator is the only one designated to exercise it.

Other authors[80] maintain that the prohibition to delegate this faculty enunciated in pre-Code law remains in force, so that delegation is ruled out unless there is explicit indication of that fact in the apostolic indult. An argument in support of this position can be formulated from the text and general tenor of canonical legislation on indulgences. Canon 721, §1 clearly declares that no association can affiliate others without an apostolic indult, because this power, with the right to delegate it, depends upon the will of the Roman Pontiff. Affiliation, in fact, effects the communication of indulgences—indeed, the power to affiliate contains within itself and primarily expresses itself through the communication of indulgences.[81] Now, according to canon 913, it is not permitted to delegate the faculty to grant indulgences, unless the indult from the Holy See expressly grants such permission.[82] By strict inference, then, the faculty to affiliate may not be delegated. For this reason apostolic indults, which grant to primary societies and to religious institutes the

[78]*De Fidelium Associationibus*, p. 70.

[79]Canon 74.

[80]Beringer, F.-Steinen, P., *Die Ablaesse*, II, n. 127; Amanieu, A., "Archiconfrérie," *DDC*, col. 944; Matthaeus a Coronata, *Institutiones*, I, p. 931; Vromant, G.-Bongaerts, L., *De Fidelium Associationibus*, p. 125 (footnote 2).

[81]Canons 722, §1 and 723, 3o.

[82]Canon 913.—"Inferiores Romano Pontifice nequeunt: 1.o Facultatem concedendi indulgentias aliis committere, nisi id eis a Sede Apostolica expresse fuerit indultum; . . ."

power to affiliate, invariably state that the affiliations must be carried out by the moderators and superiors. Affiliation cannot be effected independently of the communication of spiritual privileges and indulgences. Hence, the supreme moderator who acts in the name of the primary society cannot delegate this faculty.[83]

Article 4: Conditions Necessary for Valid Affiliation

Section 1: *Status of the Association to be Affiliated*

A: CANONICAL ESTABLISHMENT

Before proceeding to the enumeration of the conditions required for affiliation, the Code of Canon Law focuses attention upon the status of the association to be affiliated. Canon 723, 1° singles out two prerequisites: namely, the canonical establishment of the association and its non-affiliation to any other primary society.[84] These two conditions relate to the pre-affiliation status of the association in question. Both must be ascertained before and verified in the act of affiliation. If not, the attempted affiliation is null and void.

The first condition demands that the association seeking affiliation be canonically established. A number of authors interpret the words *canonice erecta* in the broadest possible meaning, so as to subsume under the terms of the canon associations which have mere ecclesiastical approbation. In other words, they would argue for the relevance of the canon to all associations possessing moral personality or ecclesiastical approbation.

The arguments advanced in support of this interpretation may be summarized as follows:

1) The text of the canon must be understood in the sense that all associations established according to the norms of the Code of Canon Law are eligible for affiliation. Canon 708 states that the approbation of the Ordinary is sufficient to qualify pious unions for the reception of spiritual favors and indulgences. Now the primary purpose of affiliation is the communication of indulgences. Furthermore, one of the most fruitful sources of spiritual favors and indulgences is the

[83]Cf. Amanieu, A., "Archiconfrérie," *DDC*, col. 944.

[84]Canon 723.—"Ad aggregationis validitatem requiritur ut: 1°. Associatio iam fuerit canonice erecta nec alii archiconfraternitati vel primariae unioni aggregata; . . ."

communication of these spiritual grants from a primary society to its affiliates.

2) Confirmation of the preceding argument is drawn from the fact that according to the canons, primary unions need not have moral personality. If moral personality is demanded in the affiliate, the situation would arise where a primary society without moral personality can affiliate pious unions only on the condition that they possess moral personality. Such an anomaly is surely not contemplated by the legislator. The interpretation is hardly reasonable that imposes greater demands upon the passive subject of affiliation than upon the active subject.[85]

3) Vermeersch-Creusen argue that affiliation properly speaking supposes the existence of an association with moral personality. Should this moral personality be lacking, the juridical status is one of collegiate affiliation to the primary society on the part of the members of the merely approved society. On this basis, the relationship of true and proper affiliation is not realized. Rather there is effected an *en masse* affiliation of the individual members of the approved society to the primary association. It makes no difference whether the primary association has moral personality or not.[86]

Contrary to this interpretation, many authors demand moral personality on the part of the association to be affiliated. They argue that the clarity of the text of canon 723 allows no other interpretation. First of all, the canon makes use of terminology so generic in character that it is all-inclusive. The word *associatio* is used advisedly, so as to include every type of ecclesiastical society. At the same time the legislator prescribes moral personality on the part of each association by using the technical phrase *canonice erecta.* It is difficult to see how he might have expressed more clearly this requirement of moral personality in an association seeking affiliation.

Prior to the Code of Canon Law, associations which desired affiliation had to be established as moral persons. Even though local Ordi-

[85]Veermersch, A.-Creusen, I., *Epitome,* I, p. 657; Schaefer, T., *De Religiosis ad Normam Codicis Iuris Canonici* (4. ed., Romae: Typis Polyglottis Vaticanis, 1947), n. 1802; Regatillo, E., *Institutiones Iuris Canonici,* n. 805; Vromant, G.-Bongaerts, L., *De Fidelium Associationibus,* p. 123.

[86]Vermeersch, A.-Creusen, I., *Epitome,* I, p. 657; *Periodica,* XVI (1927), pp. 56-58.

naries were not bound to a definite formulary in the founding of associations, they had to establish them as moral persons, as a condition for affiliation by the primary societies.[87] The Sacred Congregation always demanded moral personality as an essential requirement for the communication of indulgences and privileges.[88] In view of pre-Code legislation and the embodiment of its prescriptions in the text of the canon, it is difficult to substantiate a case for any other interpretation of the phrase *canonice erecta.* The text of the law seems beyond doubt, and recourse to the principles of canon 18 for resolving a doubt of law becomes unnecessary.

Contrary to the interpretation of Vermeersch-Creusen, it should be remarked that the Code in no place posits two types of affiliation. It merely speaks of the affiliation of an association and the communication of privileges and indulgences between the primary society and its affiliate. Members of the affiliated association share in the privileges and indulgences in question, in virtue of their membership in the affiliated association and not insofar as they are individuals affiliated to a primary union. As members of an affiliated society, they participate in all its privileges and indulgences. They do not enjoy the privileges and indulgences of the primary union. Similarly, it is unwarranted to object that, granting the requirement of moral personality in the association to be affiliated, something more is being demanded from an affiliate than from the primary union. In the final analysis, primary societies are of a different grade from that of affiliated societies, since the Holy See alone grants the rank of archconfraternity or primary union. Besides, it is by reason of an apostolic indult that the primary society affiliates, not in virtue of its internal organization.[89]

In view of the arguments adduced, it seems that the latter opinion (requiring moral personality of the association seeking affiliation)

[87]Clement VIII, const. *"Quaecumque,"* 7 dec. 1604—*Fontes,* n. 192.

[88]S. C. Indulg., *Cameracen.,* 25 ian. 1842, ad 2—*Fontes,* n. 5022; *Pinerolien.,* 12 maii 1843, ad 1—*Fontes,* n. 5030; *Cameracen.,* 25 febr. 1877—*ASS,* X (1877), 144. Cf. Beringer, F.-Steinen, P., *Die Ablaesse,* II, nn. 43, 118; Pignatelli, J., *Consultationes Canonicae* (11 vols. in 4, Coloniae Allobrogum, 1700), Tom. IV, consult. XXI, n. 3; Wernz, F., *Ius Decretalium ad usum Praelectionum in Scholis Textus Iuris Canonici sive Iuris Decretalium* (6 vols., Romae: Ex Typographia Polyglotta S. C. De Propaganda Fide, 1905-1914), III, p. 418.

[89]Cf. Seraphinus de Angelis, *De Fidelium Associationibus,* I, p. 68; Amanieu, A., "Archiconfrérie," *DDC,* col. 942; Matthaeus a Coronata, *Institutiones,* I, p. 930.

should be the accepted interpretation of canon 723, 1°. The fact that the prescription of the canon is substantially a repetition of pre-Code legislation provides the basis for its interpretation according to pre-Code authority.[90] Nevertheless, the opposite opinion is not without intrinsic arguments and weighty extrinsic authority so that it must be recognized as solidly probable.[91] And since the canon is dealing with prescriptions that effect the validity of an affiliation, the opinion is of great importance. For, when a *dubium iuris* exists in reference to invalidating laws, the rule of canon 15 applies, namely, in a positive doubt of law ecclesiastical laws (even invalidating ones) do not bind. Consequently, because of the *dubium iuris* concerning the meaning of "canonice erecta" in canon 723, 1°, an ecclesiastical society, seeking affiliation, would not have to be constituted as a moral person as a prerequisite for valid affiliation. As long as the association is ecclesiastically approved, it can validly and licitly request and receive affiliation.[92]

B: NON-AFFILIATION WITH ANOTHER PRIMARY SOCIETY

The second condition required by canon 723, 1° is the non-affiliation of the canonically established association to another archconfraternity or primary union. This, too, was a pre-Code requisite dating back to the Constitution *Quaecumque* of Clement VIII.[93] The absence of previous affiliation to another primary society is demanded as a safeguard for the communication of indulgences and spiritual privileges. If affiliation to several primary societies were allowed, one immediate result would be a confusing accumulation of indulgences. This in turn would gradually lead to a loss of appreciation for spiritual favors. To offset these contingencies, and in particular to prevent an individual association from amassing too great a number of indulgences and spiritual favors without the knowledge of the Holy See, the Code of Canon Law incorporated the old law, and hence still tolerates on the part of an

[90] Canon 6, 2°.

[91] Seraphinus de Angelis, *De Fidelium Associationibus,* I, p. 69, will not admit the probability of the opinion which holds that an approved ecclesiastical association may be affiliated, since he considers the words "canonice erecta" of the canon as certainly indicating moral personality.

[92] Cf. Vromant, G.-Bongaerts, L., *De Fidelium Associationibus,* p. 123.

[93] 7 dec. 1604—*Fontes,* n. 192; S. C. Indulg., *Urbis et Orbis,* 19 oct. 1866—*Fontes,* n. 5074.

association only a single affiliation to one primary society. If a second affiliation is attempted, the act is null and void, the original affiliation meanwhile remaining intact and with no loss of indulgences or privileges.[94]

Both of the aforementioned conditions apply to every type of ecclesiastical association seeking affiliation; namely, that the society seeking affiliation be canonically established and that it be not affiliated to another primary society. On their verification depends the validity of the affiliation. Positive doubts as to the validity of a particular affiliation should be resolved since the valid grant of indulgences depends upon it. Should the need arise, a sanation can be obtained from the Holy See.[95]

Section 2: *Written Consent and Recommendation of Local Ordinary*

Before an affiliation can be validly effected, the local Ordinary in whose jurisdiction the association is established must endorse a letter of recommendation and give his written consent to the affiliation. His testimonial letter should contain an attestation to the canonical establishment of the association, its utility, and the ability to attain its specific purpose. The letter ought to single out the piety and zeal of its members in the performance of charitable works and give evidence of the increase of membership according to the historical vicissitudes of the association. This written recommendation of the local Ordinary is necessary for validity.[96] It is not necessary that the testimonial letter and the written consent be made in two separate documents. It suffices that the letter which contains the written consent to the affiliation also commend the religious spirit of the association.[97] This written testimonial and consent of the local Ordinary must be obtained before the

[94]Canon 723, 4º states that an affiliation is perpetual.

[95]There are numerous examples of sanations granted by the Holy See in this regard. Cf. two decrees of the Sacred Congregation of Indulgences: *Urbis et Orbis*, 8 ian. 1861—*Fontes*, nn. 5061, 5062. Consult also *Aurelianen.*, 18 aug. 1868, ad 4—*Fontes*, n. 5075.

[96]Canon 723, 2º.

[97]S. C. Indulg., *Ordinis Praedicatorum*, 20 maii 1896—*Fontes*, n. 5127.

affiliation is attempted. If not previously obtained, the decree of affiliation is invalid.[98]

The proper Ordinary for issuing these documents is the local Ordinary where the association to be affiliated is established. His competence in this matter is exclusive and allows for no exception. The vicar general without a special mandate cannot validly provide either the necessary testimonial letters or the consent to the affiliation. This faculty, however, may be given to him in the concession of general power in such a manner as to cover all cases involving various affiliations.[99]

A question arises as to whether the vicar capitular can during the vacancy of the episcopal see grant letters of affiliation. Prior to the Code of Canon Law, it was disputed whether this incompetency of the vicar capitular affected the validity of the affiliation or only the liciety. In 1878 the Holy See was asked whether the vicar capitular could validly grant the necessary testimonial letters and consent for affiliation. The Sacred Congregation of Indulgences merely replied that the vicar capitular should refrain from acting in the case. The response, consequently, did not settle the dispute.[100] Canon 686, §4 asserts that the vicar capitular cannot establish associations as moral persons nor give the necessary consent for their institution or affiliation. The wording of the canon does not in itself provide a cogent argument for the nullity of a contrary act. Therefore, it may still be maintained that the vicar capitular who acts in contravention to this provision posits an illicit but not invalid act.[101]

A further question centers around associations reserved to religious and established in their own churches or oratories. If such reserved associations are established as moral persons but not *ad modum corporis organici,* may they be affiliated to the primary society without the con-

[98] S. C. Indulg., *Engolismen.*, 3 dec. 1892—*Fontes*, n. 5116.

[99] Canon 686, §4. Cf. Gougnard, A., *Tractatus de Indulgentiis* (5. ed. Mechliniae: H. Dessain, 1933), p. 153; S. C. Indulg., *Aurelianen.*, 18 aug. 1868, ad 3—*Fontes*, n. 5075.

[100] S. C. Indulg., *Congregationis Pretiosissimi Sanguinis*, "II. Utrum Vicarius Capitularis possit valide concedere litteras testimonales ac consensum requisitum a Clemente VIII pro aggregatione confraternitatum?—*Vicarius Capitularis se abstineat.*" —*Fontes*, 5085.

[101] Cf. Vromant, G.-Bongaerts, L., *De Fidelium Associationibus*, p. 25; and Matthaeus a Coronata, *Institutiones*, I, p. 891, seem to imply that the vicar capitular would act invalidly in this case.

sent and approval of the local Ordinary? Some authors,[102] arguing by analogy from canon 686, §3 are of the opinion that the recommendation and consent of the local Ordinary are not necessary for the affiliation of these associations. Since these societies do not require his consent for their establishment, *a pari* they do not require his consent and recommendation for affiliation. Furthermore, just as permission for the transferral of these reserved associations is granted by the religious superior,[103] so, too, for the affiliation of such an association the consent and approval of the local Ordinary is not required.

In opposition to this interpretation stands the clear and definite wording of canon 723. Here, the legislator is drawing up the conditions essential to every affiliation. The text and context are precise in meaning and no exception or restriction is made. Nor can any distinctions be inferred from the various terms used by the legislator. Consequently, recourse to the principle of analogy is not indicated, since such an interpretive instrument is to be employed only in case of obscure or doubtful passages.[104] Besides, the general law before the Code of Canon Law was absolute in requiring the recommendation and consent of the local Ordinary for each and every affiliation. In view of these considerations, there seems to be no solid reason for positing or presupposing a change in the law or in its interpretation.[105]

Section 3: Recognition of Indulgences and Privileges Capable of Communication

The purpose and consequence of affiliation is the communication of indulgences and privileges. To keep the procedural phases and the final effects of such an act free and clear of unnecessary legal entanglements, the legislator has determined that in the actual communication of privi-

[102]Matthaeus a Coronata, *Institutionies*, I, p. 930; Jone, H., *Commentarium in Codicem Iuris Canonici* (3 vols., Paderborn: Ferdinandus Schoeningh, 1950-1955), I, p. 627.

[103]Canon 719, §2. Cf. Jone, H., *Commentarium in Codicem Iuris Canonici*, I, p. 625.

[104]Canon 18.

[105]Canon 6, 2°. Cf. S. C. Indulg., *Urbis et Orbis*, 19 oct. 1866—*Fontes*, n. 5074. Cf. Seraphinus de Angelis, *De Fidelium Associationibus*, I, p. 69; Vromant, G.-Bongaerts, L., *De Fidelium Associationibus*, p. 123.

leges and indulgences through affiliation, a specific catalog of every spiritual benefit capable of communication be compiled. Before this list can be sent to the affiliate, the local Ordinary of the primary society must give his official recognition.[106] In effect, this regulation serves as a safeguard in eliminating privileges and indulgences which are either of doubtful origin or not properly authenticated. This examination of the authenticity of communicable favors must be carried out by the local Ordinary of the primary society. It is a condition necessary for validity of the affiliation. Obviously, the local Ordinary should take great care that the individual indulgences and privileges are properly listed before indicating approval of the document.

In every diocese, with the exception of Rome, this official inspection and recognition devolve upon the local Ordinary of the primary society. In Rome, the Cardinal Vicar is the competent authority for the authorization of such summaries of indulgences and privileges.[107] This document, once prepared, signed, and sealed, is to be forwarded to the association seeking affiliation along with the diploma of affiliation.

In the event the primary society wishes to publish the list of communicable spiritual privileges and indulgences, the legislation relevant to the publication of indulgences must be observed. The *imprimatur* of the local Ordinary is required and must appear in print at the beginning or end of the summary. The contents of the *imprimatur* must furnish the name of the local Ordinary, the seat of his jurisdiction, and the date of the granting of permission for publication. The *imprimatur* of the local Ordinary is given in writing.[108]

Section 4: *Formulary of Affiliation*

Canon 723 identifies the formulary to be used in the act of affiliation as the one prescribed in the statutes of each primary society. In the statutes of many archconfraternities and primary unions there is a specific formulary which mentions all documents affecting the society. Many even include the full text of the various grants of privileges and

106Canon 723, 3°.

107Cf. p. 79 ff. of this dissertation in determining what indulgences and privileges are to be communicated, and the appendix (page 124 ff.) for the indulgences communicated by the Primary Society of Christian Mothers.

108Canons 1388, §1 and 1394, §1.

indulgences by the Holy See. Often enough, too, one finds catalogued all the conditions for a valid affiliation as prescribed in canon 723.[109]

Prior to the Code of Canon Law, Clement VIII prescribed a standard formulary to be used by every primary society, under pain of nullity.[110] On October 19, 1866, the Sacred Congregation of Indulgences issued a new formulary and prescribed it for the validity of affiliation.[111] The obligation of following the text demanded by the Sacred Congregation applied only to the substance of the formulary.[112] As long as the formulary was not substantially altered, the act of affiliation was valid. The essential elements included the nature, purpose, and title of the primary society and of the society to be affiliated; the proper designation and respective location of the churches in which both societies were established; express mention of the conditions required by the general law for affiliation, and the signature of the official qualified to issue the document. If the same document contained the list of indulgences and privileges, their recognition by the local Ordinary had to be obtained. Each indulgence had to be mentioned separately, along with the conditions necessary for gaining it. The exact nature of the privileges also had to be included in this list, so that there would be no error in extending or limiting them. The substance of the formulary was not affected by the inclusion of relevant remarks on the origin and excellence of the primary society.[113]

The Code of Canon Law does not directly prescribe this formulary. Canon 723, 4° demands the use of a standard formulary of affiliation whenever the statutes so prescribe, and this, under pain of nullity. To determine the extent to which a formulary prescribed by statutory law must be followed, it is safe to abide by the pre-Code principle: the formulary must be followed in substance.[114]

[109]For an example of such a formulary see page 73.

[110]Clement VIII, const. *"Quaecumque,"* 7 dec. 1604—*Fontes*, n. 192.

[111]S. C. Indulg., *Urbis et Orbis*, 19 oct. 1866—*Fontes*, n. 5074.

[112]The official annotation reads: "in substantialibus quatenus non sit vetitum addere vel immutare aliqua in eadem, quae substantiam non afficiant; addendo etiam, si lubet, quae respiciunt originem, praestantiam, etc. Societatis aggregantis." *Ibidem.*

[113]*Ibidem.*

[114]Vromant, G.-Bongaerts, L., *De Fidelium Associationibus*, p. 124 (footnote 1); Seraphinus de Angelis, *De Fidelium Associationibus*, I, p. 70. The *Unio Apostolica*

For those primary societies whose statutory law does not prescribe a particular formulary, the decree of affiliation must contain such elements as are necessary to describe the act of affiliation. Consequently, the document must set forth the proper designation of the primary society and the association to be affiliated, the act of affiliation, the person exercising the faculty, the date and place of issuance and the official seal of the primary society. The document is to be accompanied by a list of the indulgences and privileges which bears the recognition of the local Ordinary. The following may serve as a formulary:

"Dilectis nobis in Christo Confratribus Societatis . . . in ecclesia . . . civitatis . . . auctoritate . . . erectae salutem in Domino sempiternam.

Nos qui iuxta officii nostri debitum fidelium salutem, pietatisque ac religionis progressum procurare debemus, libenter nostrae Archiconfraternitati alias eiusdem instituti confraternitates adiungimus et aggregamus, eisque sic aggregatis indulgentias, facultates et indulta iuxta facultatem nobis a Summis Pontificibus concessam impertimur. Qua de re cum D. . . . Confraternitatis vestrae . . . aggregationem proposuerit, nos, Supremus Moderator praedictae Archiconfraternitatis, Codici Iuris Canonici inhaerentes, his nostris litteris, praedictam confraternitatem canonice erectam, attentis consensu Ordinarii loci scriptis dato litterisque testimonialibus, quibus eius institutum, pietas et religio commendantur, nostrae Archiconfraternitati, iuxta facultatem Apostolicam nobis concessam, in perpetuum adiungimus et aggregamus, atque illi eiusque confratribus indulgentias et spirituales gratias nostrae Archiconfraternitati directe et nominatim a Sede Apostolica concessas largimur et communicamus omnes, iuxta tenorem elenchi quem rite recognitum ob Ordinario loci nostri una cum his litteris tradimus.

Quibus omnibus indulgentiis et gratiis spiritualibus ibi singulatim descriptis praedicta confraternitas potiatur et gaudeat iuxta memorati codicis canones, praesertim sequentem:

Canon 723:—Ad aggregationis validitatem requiritur ut: 1) Asso-

---

Sacerdotum founded in Paris was made a primary union by Benedict XV. However, it is to use the formulary prescribed by Clement VIII along with the amendments issued by the Sacred Congregation of Indulgences.—*AAS*, XIII (1921), 303. Pius XII raised the *Unio Excubiarum Honoris Sacratissimi et Immaculati Cordis B.M.V.* to a primary union. No special formulary is prescribed for affiliation, "servatis vero in cunctis de iure servandis."—*AAS*, XLVI (1954), 363.

ciatio iam fuerit canonice erecta nec ulli archiconfraternitati vel primariae unioni aggregata; 2) Fiat de consensu Ordinarii loci scriptis dato una cum eius litteris testimonialibus: 3) Indulgentiae, privilegia et aliae gratiae spirituales quae per aggregationem communicantur, enumerentur in elencho, ab Ordinario loci in quo Archiconfraternitas sita est, recognito et societati aggregatae tradendo; 4) Aggregatio fiat formula in statutis praescripta et in perpetuum; 5) Litterae aggregationis expediantur gratis omnino et nulla prorsus mercede etiam sponte oblata, exceptis necessariis expensis.

In quorum testimonium has litteras fieri et per nostrae Archiconfraternitatis secretarium subscribi et publicari mandavimus, sigilloque officii nostri muniri.

Datum ... die ... anni ...

L. ✠ S. Moderator Generalis

Section 5: *Gratuity of Affiliation*

The Code of Canon Law stipulates, in conjunction with the diploma of affiliation, that all affiliations must be issued *gratis*. Violation of this prescription invalidates the act of affiliation. The purpose of this law is to obviate the scandal that might easily arise were a form of donation allowed. Affiliation, it should be recalled, is basically the concession of indulgences and privileges. On that account, the danger of simony is ever present. Thus, canon 723, 5° forbids the acceptance of any offering even if made spontaneously. It is not difficult to see how a freewill offering made on such an occasion would ultimately be related to the communication of the indulgences and spiritual favors involved in the affiliation.[115] Nevertheless, canon law does permit a small fee to cover the necessary expenses. Prior to the Code of Canon Law the same prescription was strictly enforced, so that an affiliating society might only accept a small recompense to cover the cost of the writing materials and secretarial work involved. The amount fixed by the Sacred Congregation at the time was not to exceed 30 francs.[116] By reason of this

[115]Canons 727, §1 and 728.

[116]S. C. Indulg., *Urbis et Orbis*, 19 oct. 1866—*Fontes*, n. 5074: "7. Quod litterae erectionis et aggregationis gratis omnino ac nulla prorsus mercede etiam a sponte dantibus sub praetextu quoque merae eleemosynae accepta expediri et concedi possint, et solummodo titulo expensarum pro pergamena, scriptura vel impres-

pre-Code legislation and the time-honored practice of the Holy See in permitting a small fee for necessary expenses,[117] authors generally allow a fee not in excess of 30 gold francs (approximately $6 in American money).[118] In support of this opinion, the decree of the Sacred Congregation of the Council, under date of March 27, 1914, may be cited. The Sacred Congregation declared an affiliation valid if an archconfraternity or primary union charged a fixed amount of 30 gold francs for each case of affiliation, even though expenses did not actually reach that sum. The decree further proscribed under penalty of rendering the affiliation null and void the retention of any amount in excess of 30 gold francs, even if offered as alms.[119]

The exact statement of the Code deserves study: "The document of affiliation is to be issued entirely free of charge, without the acceptance of any payment whatsoever, even when spontaneously offered, except for necessary expenses."[120] As no definite sum is stipulated, the fee is to be determined on the basis of actual expenses. When authors set the amount at 30 gold francs, they are not proferring an absolute standard. This sum is based on a judgment of ordinary expenses covering all phases of the materials and effort involved. Should it transpire that the costs exceed 30 gold francs ($6), the primary society may charge more and this would not be in violation of the prescription of canon law.[121]

A further question may be asked with regard to donations made to primary societies on the occasion of affiliation but not intended as an

---

sionis stipendio, sigillorum expensis, chordulis, cera, Secretarii Notariique labore vel mercede aliisque omnibus eam quantitatem, quae non excedat summam scutatorum sex monetae Romanae in Italia, et extra Italiam non excedat summam libellarum vulgo *francs* triginta, pro singula aggregatione vel institutione sive confirmatione recipere liceat."

117 Cf. S. C. Indulg., *Urbis et Orbis,* 8 ian. 1861—*Fontes,* n. 5061.

118 Matthaeus a Coronata, *Institutiones,* I, p. 932; Seraphinus De Angelis, *De Fidelium Associationibus,* I, p. 70; Vromant, G.-Bongaerts, L., *De Fidelium Associationibus,* p. 125; Vermeersch, A.-Creusen, I., *Epitome,* I, p. 657.

119 This decree of the Sacred Congregation is cited by Beringer, F.-Steinen, P., *Die Ablaesse,* II, n. 66 (footnote 3).

120 Canon 723, 5o.

121 An offering of $5 is usually sent to the Archconfraternity of Christian Mothers, St. Augustine's Church, Pittsburgh, Pa., to defray the expenses of issuing diplomas of affiliations.

offering in payment for the affiliation. More specifically, may a primary society accept offerings made to further its charitable works, if these are made on the occasion of the affiliation? Amanieu[122] is of the opinion that an archconfraternity or primary union may, under the circumstances described, accept an alms spontaneously given, as long as it is used in connection with the specific purpose of the primary society. In defense of his opinion he argues that canon 723, 5° prohibits the acceptance of offerings, even those freely made, in conjunction with the act of affiliation. The canon makes no reference to alms given to the primary society with a view to its charitable works. Prior to the Code, the Sacred Congregation of the Council was asked whether affiliating societies were permitted, as a general rule, to ask for or accept offerings from their affiliates, in order to further the specific purpose of the primary society. The Sacred Congregation replied that as a general rule the affiliating society might not ask for such an offering. Significantly, the response did not mention anything about the acceptance of such offerings.[123]

All factors considered, however, serious objections militate against this opinion. First of all, such donations, even if offered in view of the specific purpose of the primary society, are given on the occasion of the affiliation. These surely would not have been offered had the affiliation not taken place. Actually, then, the principle of canon 730 should be applied, namely, that on the occasion of spiritual ministration an offering may be accepted if a title to it is recognized by canon law or legitimate custom. However, canon 723, 5° only recognizes the title of compensation for the necessary expenses involved in the act of affiliation and does not allow any other title on the occasion of affiliation. Furthermore, no general custom has ever been recognized by the Holy See. On the other hand, the decree of the Sacred Congregation of Indulgences which was issued on March 6, 1608 with the approval of Paul V, declared that in making affiliations, a primary society might not charge

[122] Amanieu, A., "Archiconfrérie," *DDC*, col. 944.

[123] S. C. C., 27 mart. 1914: "Quaeritur utrum generatim in erigendis seu aggregandis sodalitatibus, ut supra, licitum non sit quidem pro erectione et aggregatione ipsa sed in finem archiconfraternitatis seu sodalitatis prima-primariae a sodalitatibus noviter erectis seu aggregatis eleemosynas petere et accipere.

Resp.: Generatim Erigenti seu Aggreganti petere non licet." Cited by Beringer, F.-Steinen, P., *Die Ablaesse*, II, n. 66 (footnote 4).

more than was necessary to cover expenses (*scutatum unum aureum*). Nothing beyond this amount was to be demanded or accepted under any pretext whatsoever, and the primary society was not to receive any offering spontaneously offered by the affiliate even if tendered in the form of alms.[124] This legislation was reiterated from time to time in later decrees, and the invalidity of affiliation resulting from the violation of this law was also intermittently reasserted.[125]

In the formulary of affiliation prescribed immediately before the Code, the prohibition was reenforced with typical severity. An amount not exceeding 30 gold francs might be received by way of recompense for the expenses of affiliation. Any offering other than that was not permitted. This law was sanctioned by the penalty of nullity for the attempted affiliation.[126] Hence, a contrary custom of accepting alms on the occasion of an affiliation could not have existed prior to the Code.

In opposition to the opinion of Amanieu another noteworthy consideration may be urged. To be sure, an alms made on the occasion of affiliation would not have been made otherwise. It is definitely not the practice of an ecclesiastical society to make donations to other ecclesiastical societies since its funds are to be used for its own specific purposes. Offerings given on the occasion of affiliation can hardly be divorced from a direct casual relation to the affiliation. As such they are expressly forbidden under pain of nullifying the affiliation.[127]

One final question should be considered at this point. May primary associations receive offerings from their affiliates, not on the occasion of affiliation itself but subsequently, after the formalities of affiliation have been terminated? A theoretical case may be constructed in which the archconfraternity or primary union is in need of funds, e.g., to take on a new work or to repair its church. Would it be permissible to ask the

124S. C. Indulg., 6 mart. 1608—Ferraris, L., *Bibliotheca*, s.v. "Confraternitas," art. 1, n. 47.

125Cf. *Decreta Authentica S. C. Indulg.*, nn. 76, 80, 209.

126S. C. Indulg., *Urbis et Orbis*, 19 oct. 1866—*Fontes*, n. 5074: "7. Quod litterae erectionis et aggregationis gratis omnino ac nulla prorsus sub praetextu quoque merae eleemosynae accepta expediri et concedi possint, et solummodo titulo expensarum . . . recipere liceat."

127A rebuttal from analogy premised on Mass stipends is irrelevant. A priest has a right to sustenance and the Church has recognized and approved the custom of the faithful offering stipends for Masses in fulfillment of their obligation to support the priest. Cf. canon 824, §1.

affiliates for donations? There is no doubt that a primary society may collect and accept alms according to its statutory law,[128] in order to further its spiritual activities. However, given the concrete circumstances of the case, it is only with great subtlety that one can construe such an appeal independently of immediate reference to the act of affiliation. On this basis, it would seem that a primary society is not permitted to solicit financial aid from its affiliated associations.[129]

[128]Canon 691.

[129]Canons 686, §5, 723, 5o, 730 and 1507, §1, reveal the mind of the legislator in this matter.

CHAPTER V

EFFECTS OF AFFILIATION

The entire purpose of affiliation, as has already been indicated, is the communication of privileges and indulgences between the primary society and its affiliate. This transmission of communicable spiritual favors is a direct and necessary consequence of affiliation, irrespective of the volition of the one who issues the diploma of affiliation. The material object of this communication, its juridic properties, its permanent nature, the legal relation existing between the primary society and the affiliate are all treated *in extenso* by the Code of Canon Law, since the disposition of these matters is totally dependent upon the will of the Roman Pontiff. It is to these related areas that attention is now directed. The present chapter, under two main headings, will consider: 1) the material object and the juridical characteristics of the communication of spiritual favors between the primary society and its affiliates; and 2) the juridic relation between the primary society and its affiliates.

Article 1: The Material Object and the Juridical Characteristics of the Communication of Privileges

The juridic institute of communication as a source of privileges is treated in canon 64. Here the object of communication is restricted to privileges, that is, special normative rights created by law or by a special act of the competent superior. It cannot be held with certainty that other favorable concessions (e.g., indulgences) are implicitly contained in the term *privilegium* of canon 64. The canon refers solely, it seems, to privileges in the strict sense of the word.[1] Nevertheless, this section of the Code does set down the norms which regulate the concession of

[1]Matulenas, R., *Communication—A Source of Privileges,* The Catholic University of America, Canon Law Studies, n. 183 (Washington, D.C.: The Catholic University of America, 1943), p. 129. However, cf. G. Michiels whose much broader interpretation of the term *privilege* furnishes leeway for other spiritual favors. *Normae Generales Iuris Canonici* (2. ed., 2 vols., Tournai: Desclée et Co., 1949), II, p. 552 ff.

privileges through communication. These norms, cumulatively taken, represent a necessary standard for determining whether or not a spiritual favor is capable of communication.

While canon 64, according to the more common view, restricts the material object of communication to privileges alone, canon 722, §1 broadens the scope of the object so as to include all indulgences, privileges and other spiritual favors. It is necessary for these communicable favors to have been granted by the Holy See directly and by name. This stipulation applies not only to those which the Holy See has already granted but also to those which will be granted in the future. The general terminology of canon 722, §1, when it speaks of *all* indulgences, privileges and *other communicable favors,* points to an object of the broadest comprehension. Only one limitation is specified, and this with respect to a twofold modality: these indulgences, privileges, and communicable favors must have been granted by the Holy See directly and by name. Canon 722, §1 is found in pre-Code legislation, so that its proper understanding and interpretation are to be found within the framework of the legal enactments which antedate 1918.

The Constitution *Quaecumque* of Clement VIII furnished much-needed legislation concerning the communication of privileges between ecclesiastical associations. In this important document are found the essential conditions relative to the institute of communication. Moreover, this document determined the object of communication by its declaration that "only those privileges, indulgences, faculties, and other spiritual favors, and indults" can be communicated which have been granted to the affiliating association *"by name* and *in particular,* not however those which have been conferred through extension or communication or any other manner, nor those under a general formulary but *expressly* and *in particular."*[2] Later legislation repeatedly asserted that indulgences and privileges capable of communication between ecclesiastical associations were restricted only to those which were singly and specifically mentioned in the authentic documents. Moreover, the original grantee, the primary society, must have received them by way of direct concession from the Holy See.[3]

At the same time the decrees and decisions of the Sacred Congrega-

[2]Clement VIII, const. *"Quaecumque,"* 7 dec. 1604—*Fontes,* n. 192.

[3]S. C. Indulg., 19 mart. 1671—*Fontes,* n. 4946; S. C. Ep. et Reg., 6 febr. 1874—*ASS,* VII (1873-1874), 641-656.

tions continually insisted that the scope of communication included all privileges, indulgences, indults, favors both spiritual and temporal, provided they were not the exclusive prerogatives of the primary society.[4] As a matter of fact, many privileges and honors were granted to archconfraternities and primary unions as unique concessions. As singular prerogatives of the primary grantee, they were not subject to communication. For instance, the privilege of exposition of the Blessed Sacrament without the permission of the local Ordinary,[5] and the indult of the privileged altar,[6] were always excepted from communication, unless it was expressly mentioned in the papal document that these privileges could be communicated. The special prerogatives of primary societies situated in Rome, which enjoyed the privilege of direct submission to Cardinal Protectors, were not granted to primary societies outside of Rome, with the result that these prerogatives could not be communicated to their affiliates. The granting of such singular privileges to these primary societies in Rome was motivated by considerations of locality.[7]

The present law has incorporated practically all the former legislation. Canon 722, §1 maintains the restrictions attached to the object of communication between ecclesiastical societies. Only those indulgences, privileges, and spiritual favors obtained by direct grant from the Holy See are subject to communication. This regulation excludes any indirect concession made to a primary society, e.g., an indulgence received by communication with a religious institute or a grant received from the local Ordinary. At the same time, privileges accruing through particular law, custom, or prescription are also excluded, since the object of communication is strictly limited to those spiritual grants made directly and by name by the Holy See.[8]

4S. R. Rota, *Brixien.*, 22 iun. 1712—*ASS*, VII (1873-1874), 646; S. C. C., *Novarien.*, 3 et 24 sept. 1718—*Fontes*, n. 3174.

5S. C. C., 13 apr. 1726—Ferraris, L., *Bibliotheca*, s.v. "Confraternitas," art. 2, n. 2, ad 4.

6S. C. Indulg., 27 nov. 1764—*Decreta Authentica S. C. Indulg.*, n. 233.

7S. C. C., *Mutinen.*, 29 nov. 1762—*Thesaurus Resolutionum Sacrae Congregationis Concilii* (Romae ex Typographia Bernabo, et Lazzarini, 1739—), XXXI (1762), p. 227.

8Therefore, even if one holds the opinion that the terminology "directe . . . concessa fuerant" of canon 64 includes privileges acquired through custom and prescrip-

At this juncture a question may be raised with respect to the indulgences and spiritual favors which an ecclesiastical society acquired prior to its having attained the status of primary society. If a confraternity had been granted a number of indulgences by the Holy See before it was raised to the rank of archconfraternity, may these indulgences be communicated? This question is explicitly answered by canon 722, §1. Such indulgences and indeed all spiritual favors granted prior to and concomitantly with the society's elevation to the rank of primary society are capable of communication. The canon also points out that any spiritual favors to be granted in the future will likewise be communicated to the affiliated societies.

However, two limitations are placed by the legislator: first, these privileges and spiritual favors must of their very nature be communicable; second, the indult by which they are granted must not prevent or prohibit such communication.[9] The first condition falls within the scope of canon 64 which lays down the principles of communication. Granted that this canon deals specifically with privileges and their communicability,[10] still, canon 64 sets forth the norms for the communication of all spiritual favors, since it deals with the concept of communication as a distinct and separate method of acquiring privileges.

It was pointed out above that only indulgences, privileges, and spiritual favors directly granted and specifically named by the Holy See are the object of communication between the primary society and its affiliates. A second stipulation set down by canon 64 is that these indulgences and privileges made to the original grantee are to be perpetual. If granted only for a time, their communication is ruled out. The reason for this restriction is not so evident. Perhaps the prohibition exists because temporary spiritual favors are usually granted for special

---

tion, the opinion has no bearing upon canon 722, §1. The wording of this latter canon excludes such an opinion by using the clause, "directe et nominatim a Sancta Sede concessae fuerint vel in posterum concedantur, nisi aliud in indulto apostolico caveatur." Spiritual favors acquired through prescription or custom would not fulfill the condition of having been granted *nominatim* by the Holy See. Furthermore, the clause "nisi aliud in indulto apostolico caveatur" presupposes only grants made by apostolic indult. Cf. Matulenas, R., *Communication—A Source of Privileges*, pp. 144-146.

[9]Canon 722, §1.

[10]Cf. Matulenas, R., *Communication—A Source of Privileges*, p. 129.

conditions verified only in the selfsame subject of the grant.[11] Or perhaps the reason for the restriction is to be found in the many practical difficulties that would arise from the communication of temporary privileges and favors, since, assuming such a situation, all affiliates would have to be notified in each given instance of the change or cessation of the individual privileges.[12] Regardless of the reason, the restriction clearly excludes any indulgence, privilege, or other spiritual favor of a temporary nature from the object of communication.

To determine the perpetuity of a spiritual favor, one must employ the juridical principle of canon 70: every privilege is perpetual unless the contrary is evident. This principle also applies to grants of indulgences, indults, and other spiritual favors. Thus, the presumption is always in favor of the perpetuity of the grant. If a concession is of a temporary nature, it devolves upon the grantor to notify the grantee of that fact. It follows, then, that any temporal limitation must be clearly indicated in the wording of the apostolic indult. Conversely, grants of spiritual favors from the Holy See to ecclesiastical societies without accompanying temporal determinations are certainly perpetual.[13]

Finally, canon 64 rules out the communication of spiritual favors granted to a primary society in view of special considerations of person, place, or thing.[14] To this category of favors incapable of communication belong grants made to a primary society because of its establishment in a special church, or its promotion of a type of work peculiar to the locality in which it is situated. Similarly, a favor may be granted to a primary society by way of special recognition to individual members of the society. On the other hand, if the grant is made in view of the specific purpose of the society or is attached to works proper to the

[11]Cf. Van Hove, A., *Commentarium Lovaniense in Codicem Iuris Canonici* (1 vol. in 5 tomes, Mechliniae-Romae: H. Dessain, Tom. V, *De Privilegiis, De Dispensationibus,* 1939), p. 141.

[12]Matulenas, R., *Communication—A Source of Privileges,* p. 150.

[13]Cf. Barbosa, A., *Variae Tractationes Iuris* (5 vols. in 1, Lugduni, 1631), V, *De Dictionibus Usufrequentioribus,* dict. 254.

[14]Canon 64. "Per communicationem privilegiorum, etiam in forma aeque principali, ea tantum privilegia impertita censentur, quae directe, perpetuo et sine speciali relatione ad certum locum aut rem aut personam concessa fuerant primo privilegiario, habita etiam ratione capacitatis subiecti, cui fit communicatio."

nature of the society, it is to be regarded as capable of being communicated.[15] To cite an example, indulgences attached to feast days of the principal patrons of a primary society would apply to all the affiliates. For, although such a concession is considered to be given in behalf of the primary society, the reason underlying the grant is common to the primary society as well as to its affiliates.[16] Nevertheless, when the Holy See grants the indult of the privileged altar to a primary society, communication of this privilege is usually excluded. In spite of this usual practice, the Primary Apostolic Union of Priests, on reception of this indult by the Holy See, was permitted to communicate the privilege to the affiliates. Undoubtedly the nature and purpose of the Union influenced the Roman Pontiff to attach the privilege to the primary union itself, rather than to its proper altar or church.[17]

In ascertaining the communicability of indulgences and spiritual favors, the importance of the final clause of canon 722, §1 should not be underestimated: *nisi aliud in indulto apostolico caveatur.* Doubtless the Holy See can in individual grants and by explicit terminology qualify as incommunicable, indulgences and privileges which would otherwise be capable of communication. But such a procedure provides indirect proof that noncommunicability is the exception. In addition, such a procedure creates a presumption of law that all grants made to primary societies by the Holy See are capable of communication, unless the document contains an express prohibition. Therefore, as long as grants are specifically and directly made by the Holy See, the presumption is in favor of their communicability.

This is the significance of the proviso in canon 722, §1 which otherwise would be completely unnecessary. When the legislator states that only such spiritual favors are subject to communication as have been directly and individually designated in a direct grant from the Holy See, the clause "unless the apostolic indult states otherwise" is implicitly understood. However, its insertion at this point helps to clarify two things. For one thing, it confirms the older legislation which specified that communication among ecclesiastical societies was conditioned

[15]Cf. S. C. Ep. et Reg., *Iurium et Privilegiorum,* 6 febr. 1874—*ASS,* VII (1873-1874), 655.

[16]Cf. the list of indulgences granted to the primary society of Christian Mothers which are communicated to its affiliates, p. 124 ff.

[17]Benedict XV, 17 apr. 1921—*AAS,* XIII (1921), 302.

by two factors: explicit designation of the privilege and direct concession by the Holy See. Secondly, it establishes the presumption, once the foregoing conditions are fulfilled, that the concession is communicable.

In the light of the preceding discussion, the conditions of noncommunicability set forth by canon 64 must be proved with certainty in order to establish an exception against canon 722, §1. The method of procedure may be formulated thus: when the requirements of canon 722, §1 are fulfilled, communicability of a spiritual benefit is the general rule, exceptions bear the burden of unequivocal proof. In other words, it must be established beyond a doubt that a given indulgence or privilege granted directly and explicitly by the Holy See, is incapable of being communicated by reason of a special relation to a person, place or thing. Anything less than certainty will not permit an inference in behalf of noncommunicability.[18]

Without belaboring the obvious, some privileges may not be communicated by a primary society because its concession or motivation relates to highly individualistic factors. For example, the faculty to affiliate and the right of precedence are prerogatives enjoyed only by primary unions and archconfraternities. Being by their very nature strictly personal, these two privileges bear a special relation to the moral subject in whom they adhere, namely the primary society. In view of that fact, they fall under the restrictions of canon 64.

The Code of Canon Law in one respect has deviated from earlier legislation. Canon 722, §1 explicitly mentions *spiritual* favors to the exclusion of temporal ones. Prior to the Code of Canon Law, the Sacred Rota in its decision of June 22, 1712, pointed out that all privileges, indults, and favors, both spiritual and temporal, are communicated by means of affiliation.[19] The present law, by contrast, restricts the object of communication to spiritual favors.

[18]Cf. Matulenas, R., *Communication—A Source of Privileges,* pp. 163-164; Michiels, G., *Normae Generales Iuris Canonici,* II, pp. 558-559.

[19]This decision is cited by A. Tachy, *Traité des Confréries,* p. 176 (footnote 2).

Article 2: The Relation of the Primary Society to Its Affiliates

Section 1: The Nature of the Juridical Bond Between the Primary Society and Its Affiliates

The act of affiliation establishes a moral bond between the primary society and its affiliates. This moral bond functions as the medium of communication for all favors subject to that process. This is not a jurisdictional relationship, since the status of affiliation and the ensuing communication do not provide a legal substratum for the exercise of power. Each ecclesiastical association with respect to its government is independent of every other ecclesiastical association, and is subject directly to the vigilance and jurisdiction of the local Ordinary.[20] Through affiliation, then, the primary society does not acquire any authority over its affiliates. Just as the primary society has no right to limit the object of communication—all spiritual favors must be communicated unconditionally—so, too, it does not acquire any right to modify, condition, or terminate the communication once it is made. Affiliation and the consequent communication are perpetual and independent of any authority inferior to the Holy See.[21]

However, granted the modality in which the indulgences and privileges transmitted through affiliation are possessed, there is a definite relation established between the primary society and its affiliates. The former obtains its grants through a direct and immediate concession while the latter receive their grants through an indirect and mediate concession. Although the affiliation does not change the juridic status of either the primary society or its affiliates, it does create the medium by which grants possessed by the primary society are transferred to its affiliates.

Section 2: The Accessory Form of Communication Between a Primary Society and Its Affiliates

The Code of Canon Law does not describe the particular form of communication which takes place between the primary society and its affiliates. Nevertheless, the text of canon 722 presupposes not only the concept of communication but also the method in which it is effected.

[20] Canon 690.

[21] Canons 722, §2 and 723, 4°. Cf. S. C. Indulg., 2 mart. 1748—*Fontes*, n. 4973.

And, in fact, while canon 64 states the essential elements of the institute of communication, canon 65 distinguishes the two methods in which communication is effected: namely, by way of equal or accessory communication.[22]

A: COMMUNICATION OF PRIVILEGES IN FORMA AEQUE PRINCIPALI

In the granting of privileges by communication *in forma aeque principali,* the increase, diminution, or loss of the privileges on the part of the primary grantee in no way affects the privileges acquired by others through their union with this common, underlying source. The privileges of the original beneficiary transmitted through equal communication become automatically the possession of the secondary beneficiary. In this way, both the primary and secondary grantee equally enjoy the privileges in question, so that both have absolute ownership, completely independent of subsequent modifications of the other's privileges. Through communication *in forma aeque principali,* therefore, the privilege remains unaffected by any variation which may affect the same privilege in the original grantee.[23]

B: COMMUNICATION OF PRIVILEGES IN FORMA ACCESSORIA

The second way of communication is *in forma accessoria.* This method of communication is based on the juridical principle: anything of an accessory nature is subject to the same consequences which affect the principle to which it adheres.[24] Accordingly, a privilege which is acquired in the accessory manner is not divisible from the privilege of the

[22]Canon 65.—"Cum privilegia acquiruntur per communicationem in forma accessoria, augentur, imminuuntur vel amittuntur ipso facto, si forte augeantur, imminuantur vel cessent in principali privilegiario; secus si acquirantur per communicationem in forma aeque principali."

[23]Cf. Matulenas, R., *Communication—A Source of Privileges,* pp. 185-190; Van Hove, A., *Commentarium Lovaniense in Codicem Iuris Canonici,* Tom. V, *De Privilegiis,* p. 142.

[24]Reg. 42, R. J. in VI°: *Accessorium naturam sequi congruit principalis,*— Reiffenstuel, A., *Ius Canonicum Universum,* Vol. VI, *Tractatus de Regulis Iuris* (Romae: 1834), 73: "Tanta est dependentia accessorii a principali, ut, regulariter loquendo, inducto, concesso, prohibito, annulato, sublato, vel confirmato principali, inductum, concessum, prohibitum, annulatum, sublatum, vel confirmatum, etiam censeatur accessorium."

principal. It is subject to the consequences which affect the permanence of the privilege conferred upon the original grantee. As a matter of fact, the Code of Canon Law explicitly points out that any modification in the privilege of the primary beneficiary (whether increase, decrease, or complete loss), will effect a corresponding alteration in the privilege which has been communicated to, and is in the actual possession of, the accessory. This fact has prompted many authors to argue from accessory communication to a position which would view the principal and accessory as possessors of a privilege that is at once specifically one and inherently the same.[25] Such an inference would make accessory communication the extension or application of a determined privilege to another subject in view of a juridical bond existing between the primary and secondary grantee.

The immediate juridic effect of accessory communication is a transmission of the favor, in virtue of which the secondary beneficiaries enjoy the favor under the same terms and conditions which apply to the principal. Likewise, any later provisions modifying the privilege of the principal automatically affect that of the accessory. The converse would not be true, because the modality of possession in the primary grantee depends solely on the will of the grantor, whereas in the accessory the modality of possession is dependent not only on the will of the grantor but also on the condition of the privilege in the principal. As a result, the communicated favor remains a single, indivisible juridic entity yet directly subject to the original beneficiary. Only such acts as are directed immediately to him or posited by him affect the status of the grant. Accordingly, only he can legitimately renounce the privilege.[26] He alone can be deprived of it owing to an abuse for which he himself is responsible.[27]

Important as it is to distinguish the notion of absolute ownership as enjoyed by the principal from the relative ownership of the accessory, it is more important still to keep distinct the use of the privilege as exercised by the principal and by the accessory. The primary grantee exercises complete control over the privilege, in as much as he alone can

[25]Suarez, *De Legibus,* l. VIII, c. 16, nn. 11 and 12; Michiels, G., *Normae Generales Iuris Canonici,* II, p. 543 ff.; Matulenas, R., *Communication—A Source of Privileges,* p. 171 ff.

[26]Canon 72.

[27]Canon 78.

gain an increment or suffer a diminution or undergo complete loss of the same. The primary grantee alone can bring about a cessation of the privilege by nonuse, contrary use, or legitimate renunciation.[28] However, the principal has no direct control over the exercise of the privilege by the accessories in virtue of the simple fact of communication. For the use of the privilege by the accessory is independent of the principal. A form of direct control in this matter can only accrue to the principal from another source, e.g., jurisdiction in disciplinary and administrative matters exercised by religious orders over other religious institutes affiliated to them. Accordingly, even though the accessory is completely dependent on the principal for the existence, nature, and condition of the communicated favor, the former is not dependent on the principal in the use and exercise of the favor by the mere fact of communication. Any restriction attached to the use of a communicated privilege must have another juridical factor as its basis.[29]

The concept of communication found in canons 64 and 65 is to be applied to the communication of indulgences, privileges and other favors expressly mentioned in canon 722, §1.[30] Canonists are unanimous in referring the communication spoken of in canon 722, §1 to the category of accessory communication.[31] Although the Code of Canon Law does not expressly identify the form of communication which obtains between the affiliated association and the primary society, it can be inferred that the accessory form is involved. In the first place, even though the primary society and its affiliates are distinct juridic personalities, there is an interdependence by reason of the act of affiliation through which the communication is made. Furthermore, the affiliated societies

[28]Canons 76; 72, §1, 3, 4. Competent authority, of course, can modify the grant of the primary beneficiary without modifying that of the accessory.

[29]Cf. Matulenas, R., *Communication—A Source of Privileges,* p. 180 ff.

[30]Those authors, whose generic interpretation of the term *privilege* in canons 64 and 65 would include other communicable favors, point out that 722, §1 is an application of the foregoing canons. Cf. Michiels, G., *Normae Generales Iuris Canonici,* II, p. 552.

[31]Michiels, G., *Normae Generales Iuris Canonici,* II, p. 543; Matulenas, R., *Communication—A Source of Privileges,* p. 181; Van Hove, A., *De Privilegiis,* p. 144; Vasto, B., *De Communicatione Privilegiorum praesertim inter Religiones* (Italia: Aquilae in Vestinis, 1936), p. 53; Vromant, G.-Bongaerts, L., *De Fidelium Associationibus,* p. 122 (footnote 3); Seraphinus de Angelis, *De Fidelium Associationibus,* I, p. 68.

depend upon the primary society for grants of future favors through communication. A new concession or the enlargement of a present one is *ipso iure* transmitted to the affiliates. All of which evidence indicates that the affiliated associations are in the condition of accessories.[32]

In pointing out that a primary society acquires no right over its affiliates through the act of communication,[33] the canon does not refute or undermine the position just established. As a matter of fact, the Code of Canon Law actually presupposes accessory communication by acknowledging a juridic relation between a primary society and its affiliates. More conclusively, the law *expressly* singles out an objective relationship in canon 723, 1°, which nullifies an attempt on the part of an affiliated association to affiliate with another primary society. This bond between the primary society and its affiliates is indispensable for communication and is of a perpetual character. As such, it points to the permanent accessory status of the affiliated organizations which acquire and possess further grants of communicable favors in virtue of their affiliation with the primary society.

A decree of the Sacred Congregation of Indulgences may be cited in confirmation of this interpretation. This decision involved the transferral of a Belgian archconfraternity to Rome by Leo XIII and its unification there with an already existing archconfraternity. The Holy Father amalgamated these two primary societies with the proviso that every communication of indulgences and privileges already made to affiliates was henceforth to be regarded as having been made by the new primary society. Upon this new primary society the Holy Father conferred the faculty to affiliate.[34] From this case it is clear that every communication of privileges and indulgences made prior to the unification of the two archconfraternities was contingent upon and conditioned by affiliation. By the very nature of the situation once the primary societies (the principals) ceased to exist, their former affiliates (the accessories) would have been deprived of the communicated favors. This consequence was

[32]Canon 722, §1.

[33]Canon 722, §2.

[34]"...Indulgentiarum vero et privilegiorum communicationes, quae confraternitatibus aggregatis hactenus factae sunt, tamquam ab hac sic unita factae habeantur. Huic tandem archisodalitati quae in unum coluit, Eadem Sanctitas Sua (Leo XIII) facultatem tribuit... aggregandi..." *ASS*, XI (1878-1879), 608.

forestalled by the will of the supreme legislator through a formal re-affiliation of all former affiliates to the new archconfraternity.[35]

Section 3: Communication of Privileges Received After Affiliation

One more point should be underscored with respect to new grants of privileges. If, after affiliation, a new grant of communicable indulgences or privileges is made to the primary society, a reaffiliation is not necessary to communicate these favors. An automatic transferral is in effect. The primary society must notify its affiliates of the new grant by a description of the indulgences and privileges together with the necessary conditions for gaining them. Special authorization by the local Ordinary of this summary of indulgences and privileges is necessary for validity before it may be sent to the affiliates.[36]

Affiliated associations always remain in the position of accessories with respect to grants made to their primary society. However, a question arises concerning indulgences which associations have enjoyed prior to affiliation to a primary society. Are these forfeited in the act of affiliation, or do they continue in effect even after affiliation has occurred?

Many authors,[37] basing their opinions on two decrees of the Sacred Congregation of Indulgences, contend that all indulgences, privileges, and other spiritual favors, obtained by an association before its affiliation, are lost in the act of affiliation. The first decree, dated May 8, 1713,

[35]Matulenas, R., *Communication—A Source of Privileges*, p. 182, footnote 42, in his treatment of accessory communication between primary societies and their affiliates, adduces as a premise: "The aggregated society not only acquires its privileges through the aggregating society, but also its existence as a juridic person." The latter part of this assertion is definitely misleading. The competency to establish ecclesiastical societies as moral persons inheres in the Holy Father, in the local Ordinaries, and for special kinds of associations in some Superior Generals of religious institutes (canon 676, §2). Archconfraternities and primary unions have the faculty to affiliate ecclesiastical societies already canonically established (canon 723, §1). If they have the power to establish ecclesiastical societies, this can only have derived from a distinct grant by the Holy See, as it is assuredly not included in the faculty of affiliation.

[36]Canon 723, 3°. Cf. p. 70 ff. of this dissertation.

[37]Vromant, G.-Bongaerts, L., *De Fidelium Associationibus*, p. 119; Ferreres, J., *Las Confradías y Congregaciones Eclesiásticas según la disciplina vigente* (Barcelona: Gustavo Gili, 1907), n. 84.

concerned a confraternity which had acquired indulgences from Pope Paul V. In this grant of indulgences there occurred the restrictive clause: "volumus autem ut si dicta sodalitas alicui archisodalitati aggregata iam sit, vel in posterum aggregetur, aut quavis alia ratione uniatur, vel etiam quomodolibet instituatur, *priores et quaevis aliae litterae Apostolicae illis nullatenus suffragentur, sed ex tunc eo ipso nullae sunt*" (italics supplied). Subsequently, the confraternity was affiliated to a primary society in Rome and the communication of indulgences followed *ipso facto*. The Holy See was asked as to the status of indulgences. The Sacred Congregation of Indulgences replied that the confraternity enjoyed only those indulgences which were communicated by virtue of the affiliation.[38]

An analogous case, involving the same restrictive clause in the original grant of indulgences, was similarly resolved by the same Congregation, on Jan. 12, 1717. The confraternity in question was later affiliated to a Roman archconfraternity. Wishing to revert to the status which obtained under the original grant of indulgences, the affiliated confraternity asked if an annulment of the affiliation were necessary to resuscitate the original grant of indulgences forfeited through affiliation. The Sacred Congregation replied that the affiliation had annulled the original grant of indulgences, and accordingly it would require renewal.[39] Vromant chooses to interpret these two decrees as indicative of the ordinary practice of the Holy See in granting indulgences.[40] Accordingly, all indulgences acquired from the Holy See prior to affiliation, are forfeited in the act of affiliation unless the apostolic indult setting forth the original grant contains an excepting clause.

However, several authors,[41] defend the opposite opinion: that is, despite the absence of an excepting clause, grants of indulgences and spiritual favors made by the Holy See to an association prior to affiliation stand unimpaired. Tachy[42] cites the decree of the Sacred Congregation of Indulgences, issued on January 30, 1843, in support of his

[38]*Decreta Authentica S. C. Indulg.*, n. 48.

[39]*Decreta Authentica S. C. Indulg.*, n. 64.

[40]Vromant, G.-Bongaerts, L., *De Fidelium Associationibus*, p. 119.

[41]Tachy, A., *Traité des Confréries*, p. 183; Seraphinus de Angelis, *De Fidelium Associationibus*, I, p. 68; Matthaeus a Coronata, *Institutiones*, I, p. 930; Amanieu, A., "Archiconfrérie," *DDC*, col. 946.

[42]*Traité des Confréries*, p. 183.

opinion. This decree clearly states that later grants of indulgences do not affect anterior ones as long as no restriction is found in the indult.[43]

This opinion does not conflict with the principles of the Code of Canon Law. Rescripts are to be understood according to the proper meaning of the words and common usage, and are not to be extended to cases other than those expressed in the rescripts.[44] But to postulate an implicit nullifying clause in such circumstances is surely an extension of the meaning. Furthermore, privileges are to be considered perpetual unless the contrary is evident.[45] The revocation or expiration of a privilege must be clearly stated in the document; otherwise, once granted, there is no challenging the fact that it remains in force.

A corroborating argument may be gathered from canon 913, 3º which deals with the granting of indulgences. By the terms of this canon no one, except the Supreme Pontiff, may attach additional indulgences to the pious works of an association which already enjoys indulgences from the Holy See or other competent authority, unless the fulfillment of new conditions is prescribed.[46] The legislator here definitely allows qualified associations to obtain indulgences not only by a direct grant from the Holy See but also from Ordinaries and others possessing proper faculties. With the exceptions of the Holy See, every competent grantor must condition the gaining of these additional indulgences upon the performance of a different work. Negatively, therefore, the canon supposes that grants from the Holy See as well as those established by canon law are not subject to this prohibition. Thus, the communication of indulgences and privileges through affiliation is effected immediately in virtue of canon 722 and consequently not subject to the prohibition of canon 913.

The formulation of canon 913, it is to be observed, warrants another

[43] *Decreta Authentica S. C. Indulg.*, n. 314: "Standum esse verbis indulti, ex quo si nulla sit expressa conditio, v. gr. *dummodo nulla alia indulgentia reperiatur concessa,* aut similia, etc., eruitur firmas remanere singulas indulgentias etiam praecedenti tempore elargitas, de quibus mentio quoque fit apud auctores de indulgentiis tractantes."

[44] Canon 49.

[45] Canon 71.

[46] Canon 913.—"Inferiores Romano Pontifice nequeunt: . . . 3º. Eidem rei seu actui pietatis vel sodalitio, cui iam a Sede Apostolica vel ab alio indulgentiae concessae sint, alias adiungere, nisi novae conditiones adimplendae praescribatur."

inference. The prohibition in question is aimed at a subsequent grant of indulgences made with respect to the same object, or act of piety, or conferred upon an association that has already received an earlier grant. It may be concluded, then, that grants of the very same indulgences made prior to affiliation remain in effect. This interpretation is well within the meaning of the law and is in complete harmony with the decrees of the Sacred Congregation of Indulgences on which the law is based.[47]

The sequence of this argumentation represents, it would seem, a strong case for the position that indulgences, privileges, and any other spiritual favors which an association enjoyed prior to affiliation remain in effect after affiliation. It makes no difference whether these indulgences and privileges were granted by the Holy See or a subordinate authority, provided the benefits in question were validly obtained. There is actually no exception to this rule. Even when a second affiliation is attempted, the Code of Canon Law nullifies this latter act, with the result that the communication of privileges originally effected remains unaltered.[48] Needless to say, a second communication of privileges is impossible. This point of law is found in papal indults, containing grants of indulgences. In fact, the Code of Canon Law incorporated it in canon 723, 1°, even though it excluded other invalidating conditions represented by the restrictive clause usually found in papal indults.[49]

In conclusion, the granting of indulgences, privileges, and any other spiritual favors by the Holy See is subject only to such limitations as are expressly stated in the indult. In the absence of a clause to the contrary, the grant must be considered absolute and perpetual.[50]

[47] S. C. Indulg., *Massilien.*, 17 dec. 1838—*Fontes*, n. 5009; *Quiten.*, 12 ian. 1878—*Fontes*, n. 5081. These two decrees repeat the prohibition upon which the Holy See has always strongly insisted: namely, no one, except the Roman Pontiff, can grant indulgences to a society which already enjoys a concession from a Bishop or the Holy See, unless accompanied by newly prescribed conditions for the gaining of the indulgences. Cf. Conc. Trident., sess. XXV, *decret. de indulg.*

[48] Cf. canon 723, 1°.

[49] Cf. p. 125 of this dissertation for the wording of the restrictive clause generally employed in the indults.

[50] Canons 39, 49, 62 and 70.

CHAPTER VI

PRECEDENCE OF PRIMARY SOCIETIES

Article 1: General Principles of Precedence

Section 1: *Concept and Purpose of Precedence*

Canonical precedence may be defined as the right of a physical or moral person to a place of honor superior in dignity to that given to others in public ecclesiastical functions. Of itself the term *precedence* may prove misleading if understood in the strictly material sense of going before another. Such a notion is far too restricted for juridic purposes. Precedence as a legal institute applies to every situation where order demands that one hold a position of dignity and honor over another.[1] For instance, the position of honor is usually relegated to the end of a procession. But at times, e.g., in the *Corpus Christi* procession, proximity to the Blessed Sacrament determines the higher places of honor and dignity. On the other hand, in the signing of public documents those of higher dignity will sign first, since the order of precedence is determined by priority of the inscription (physical position) of the signatures. Accordingly, the nature of the public function and prevailing conditions and circumstances, determine the external manifestation of precedence. If the position of highest honor is assigned to first place, then a descending arrangement of places of dignity will be followed. If the place of highest honor is at the end, an ascending arrangement of places will determine precedence.

The Code of Canon Law has set down definite norms to determine which persons have the right of precedence over others. The primary purpose of these regulations is to ensure good order in ecclesiastical functions, and to safeguard the honor and respect due to persons of higher dignity. The hierarchical nature of the church demands a correct placement of her members, so that due reverence and respect may

[1]Cf. Michiels, G., *De Personis*, p. 682; Schreiber, P., *Canonical Precedence*, The Catholic University of America Canon Law Studies, n. 408 (Washington, D.C.: The Catholic University of America Press, 1959), p. 73 (hereafter cited: *Canonical Precedence*).

be shown to those in positions of authority and higher dignity. Accordingly, the laws of precedence are based on the fundamental obligation of inferiors to manifest honor to those who are superior in authority and dignity.

Section 2: *Principles of Precedence*

The right of precedence may have authority as its immediate legal basis. Those who exercise authority over a physical or moral person have the right to precede that person.[2] This principle is based upon the subordination of a subject to his superior. In particular, this authority assumes the form of jurisdiction, as in the case of a local Ordinary with respect to his subjects. Or it may take the form of dominative power, as in the case of religious superiors with respect to their subjects. Or, finally, it may be a matter of merely private authority, as in the case of the head of an ecclesiastical association over its members. In all three instances the right of precedence is directly based on the right of authority.[3]

However, many public ecclesiastical functions demand a correct placement of persons which cannot be determined according to the principle of authority. In these cases there is no relation of subject and superior among the persons involved. By way of solution, the Code of Canon Law lays down two sets of principles. The first applies in cases involving physical persons. These norms are based on superiority of grade or rank, orders, and age.[4] The other set of regulations applies to moral persons. As such, it has special reference to ecclesiastical associations. In canon 106, 5° the legislator offers the rules of precedence governing all moral persons of the same grade and rank.[5] This canon lays down

[2]Canon 106, 2°.

[3]Cf. Schreiber, P., *Canonical Precedence,* p. 109 ff.; Michiels, G., *De Personis,* p. 686.

[4]Canon 106, 3°. Cf. Schreiber, P., *Canonical Precedence,* p. 123 ff., who gives an excellent exposition of these principles and their practical application to particular circumstances.

[5]Canon 106, 5°: "Inter varias personas morales eiusdem speciei et gradus, illa praecedit quae est in pacifica quasi-possessione praecedentiae et, si de hoc non constet, quae prius in loco, ubi quaestio oritur, instituta est; inter sodales vero alicujus collegii, ius praecedentiae determinetur ex propriis legitimis constitutionibus; secus ex legitima consuetudine; qua deficiente, ex praescripto iuris communis."

general norms to regulate precedence among moral persons who have the same juridical nature. At the same time it presupposes more specific legislation that will regulate precedence among moral persons of different grades and ranks. As a matter of fact, various sections of the Code describe three different classes of moral persons with their more specific legislation concerning precedence. The chapter of canons, religious institutes, and ecclesiastical associations of the faithful have further regulations on the matter of precedence.[6] Each of these classes has special canonical principles governing precedence, in addition to those laid down in canon 106. In the case of ecclesiastical associations of the faithful, canon 701 establishes the order of precedence among various kinds of ecclesiastical associations. For the sake of clarity the norms of canon 701 will be treated first. Since canon 106, 5° and 6°, deals with precedence among associations of the same kind and rank, it will be treated as a corollary of canon 701.

Article 2: Precedence Among Ecclesiastical Associations

Section 1: *Precedence Among Various Kinds and Grades*

There are three classes or kinds of ecclesiastical associations considered by the Code of Canon Law: third orders secular, confraternities, and pious unions.[7] This fundamental division of ecclesiastical societies serves as the basis for precedence. To avoid confusion it should be kept in mind that the legislator uses the term *association* as the equivalent of a genus under which three species are subsumed: third orders secular, confraternities, and pious unions. The Code of Canon Law leaves no room for doubt on this point, so lucidly is it expressed in canon 700 immediately prior to its treatment of the norms for precedence.

By way of introduction to the basic norms set down by canon 701, the fact should be emphasized that these laws apply only to ecclesiastical associations. Merely recommended lay societies not having ecclesiastical approval are not included in ecclesiastical precedence, since they are not true ecclesiastical societies. At the same time it might be remarked that the canon speaks of ecclesiastical associations of laymen. Because a con-

[6]Canons 408, 491, 701.

[7]Canon 700: Triplex distinguitur in Ecclesia associationum species: *tertii Ordines saeculares, confraternitates, piae uniones.*

fraternity or society of priests or clerics is not governed by the principles enunciated in this canon, another fundamental principle must be invoked in this latter instance: the clergy always precede the laity.[8]

One last preliminary question should be treated before interpreting the canon itself. This deals with the matter of precedence among ecclesiastical associations having only women as members. Authors[9] who treat this question point out that ecclesiastical associations of women may not actively participate in processions, and on that account precedence, strictly so called, cannot be applied to them. However, according to the decrees of the Sacred Congregations,[10] associations of women may be admitted to the extra-liturgical part of a procession. In view of that fact, the rules of precedence may be applied to them by analogy. Such analogical application of the norms of precedence to ecclesiastical associations of women may be employed in every case involving precedence and should not be restricted to processions. Any public function which entails the proper placement of associations of women should adhere to the norms established in the canon, as long as associations of men precede them.[11]

Canon 701, §1 establishes the general order of precedence among ecclesiastical associations of laymen as follows:

1) Third Orders Secular,
2) Archconfraternities,
3) Confraternities,
4) Primary Pious Unions (archsodalities),
5) Other Pious Unions (sodalities).

This order takes cognizance of the three basic kinds of ecclesiastical societies and draws up the positions of honor accordingly. Third orders secular precede all other ecclesiastical societies. This was the provision

[8]Canon 491.

[9]Seraphinus de Angelis, *De Fidelium Associationibus,* I, p. 39; Matthaeus a Coronata, *Institutiones,* I, p. 910; Goyeneche, S., *Quaestiones Canonicae de Iure Religiosorum* (2 vols., Neapoli: M. D'Auria Pontificius Editor, 1954-1955), II, p. 233.

[10]Cf. S. C. Ep. et Reg., *Salernitana,* 26 mart. 1897—*ASS,* XXIX (1896-1897), 627; S. R. C., 29 nov. 1901—*ASS,* XXXIV (1901-1902), 375.

[11]For instance, a sodality of the third order secular composed entirely of women should precede the primary union of Christian mothers. The latter, in turn, precede other associations of women. Cf. *Il Monitore Ecclesiastico* (Romae: Desclée, 1876—), XXVIII (1915), p. 200.

of pre-Code legislation, according to which they were always awarded first place.[12] Confraternities, in turn, enjoy the right of precedence over pious unions. The reason for this lies in the fact that confraternities have a higher purpose, namely, the promotion of public worship. The law gives special recognition to confraternities by awarding the right of precedence.

Furthermore, in canon 701, §1 the legislator singles out the rank of primary society. Archconfraternities precede confraternities, while primary unions precede pious unions. These primary societies are of a higher rank owing to their greater dignity. Immediately before the publication of the Code, the Sacred Roman Rota rendered two decisions in which they disallowed the title of greater dignity as a source of precedence.[13] The Rotal judges insisted that the *Exposcit* of Gregory XIII represented the general law which determined precedence among ecclesiastical associations.[14] The constitution of Gregory XIII did not recognize the dignity of archconfraternity or primary union as a basis for precedence. And the Sacred Rota argued that earlier decisions issued by the various Congregations in favor of primary societies were not made in view of their dignity as primary societies but in view of particular custom or priority of establishment as ecclesiastical associations.

However, on April 13, 1935, in a case of precedence between a confraternity and an archconfraternity, the Sacred Congregation of the Council asserted that the canonical principle of dignity regarding precedence among ecclesiastical associations was not a new law and had been accorded legal recognition in pre-Code decisions.[15] The Sacred Congregation cited two decisions by the Sacred Congregation of Rites in which precedence had been awarded to primary societies because of a higher grade of dignity.[16] Be that as it may, the Code of Canon Law clearly distinguishes kind and rank among ecclesiastical associations and grants the right of precedence to those of a higher rank.

[12] S. R. C., 28 maii 1886—*Fontes*, n. 6175; *Lucerina*, 4 iul. 1887—*Fontes*, n. 6183.

[13] S. R. R., *Beneventana*, 4 ian. 1915—*AAS*, VII (1915), 151-161; *Beneventana*, 13 aug. 1915—*AAS*, VIII (1916), 120-131.

[14] Gregory XIII, const. "*Exposcit*," 15 iul. 1583—*Fontes*, n. 151.

[15] S. C. C., 13 apr. 1935—*AAS*, XXIX (1937), 33-34.

[16] S. R. C., *Lucerina*, 25 sept. 1875—*Fontes*, n. 6081; *Abellinen.*, 18 aug. 1877—*Fontes*, n. 6103. A. Tachy (pre-Code author) in his work, *Traité des Confréries*, also held that primary societies had precedence over others, p. 465.

For the sake of orderly procedure, it may be well to arrange the various principles in order of application. The first principle looks to the kind of association. Third orders secular precede every other class of associations. Confraternities precede all pious unions, whether of the rank of primary union or not. Here, then, is the first principle for determining the order of precedence. An exception allowing confraternities of the Most Blessed Sacrament to precede all other confraternities and archconfraternities during processions of the Most Blessed Sacrament will be treated shortly.[17]

The second principle relates to rank within a kind of ecclesiastical society. Among confraternities the archconfraternity has the right of precedence. Among pious unions the archsodality or primary union has the right. Since sodalities, as defined by canon 707, §1, are of the same kind as pious unions, archsodalities are of the same rank as primary unions. The legislator does not draw a distinction between sodalities and pious unions in the matter of precedence, for which reason both types of societies must be listed together as forming one kind of ecclesiastical association. Archsodalities thereby fall into the same class as primary unions.[18]

An exception to these two principles must be made in processions of the Most Blessed Sacrament. The confraternity of the Blessed Sacrament takes precedence over all archconfraternities during a procession in which the Blessed Sacrament is being carried.[19] This special concession of precedence is motivated by the purpose of Blessed Sacrament confraternities. It is their particular objective to promote special devotion to the Holy Eucharist. As such, they are to be preferred above all other confraternities and pious unions and to be assigned the highest place of honor in processions of the Blessed Sacrament. However, as already indicated, they do not precede third orders secular.[20]

The same privilege of precedence seems to hold for sodalities and pious unions of the Blessed Sacrament.[21] Since these organizations have been instituted for the promotion of devotion to the Holy Eucha-

[17]Cf. canon 701, §2.

[18]Canon 700.

[19]Canon 701, §2.

[20]Canon 701. Cf. Bassi, J., *De Sodalitiis,* quaest. II, n. 51.

[21]Cf. Vermeersch, A., *Periodica,* XVI, p. 59, who proposes this opinion.

rist, it is fitting that they occupy the place of honor when performing a work that is proper to them.[22]

However, the wording of canon 701 is clear in its statement of the principle of precedence by reason of difference in kind. On the basis of this principle, all confraternities have the right to precede all pious unions. By way of further determination and limitation, canon 701, §2 states that all confraternities of the Blessed Sacrament, while in procession with the Holy Eucharist, have the right of precedence. Nothing is said about a sodality or pious union of the Blessed Sacrament. The legislator uses the term *confraternity* and not the more general designations *association* or *society*. Consequently, the technical term *confraternity* should not be extended so as to include sodality and pious union.[23]

Section 2: Precedence Among Archconfraternities and Primary Unions

In dealing with the order of precedence among various archconfraternities or primary unions, the legislator applies the principle of peaceful possession enunciated in canon 106, 5°. The canon explicitly deals with moral persons of the same class and rank. Therefore it lays down the norms for precedence among a number of archconfraternities or a

[22] PCI, 6 mart. 1927—*AAS*, XIX (1927), 161, allowed the establishment of a sodality or pious union of the Blessed Sacrament instead of a confraternity as prescribed by canon 711, §2. Cf. also canon 555 of the Oriental Code of Canon Law (Motu Proprio *Cleri Sanctitati*).

[23] Because the Pontifical Commission for the Interpretation of the Code of Canon Law permits a sodality or pious union to be established in a parish in place of a confraternity of the Most Blessed Sacrament, one may not argue to the confirmation of the opinion advanced by Vermeersch. The Oriental Code (Motu Proprio *Cleri Sanctitati*) embodies this very same legislation in canon 555, which grants to the local Ordinaries of the Oriental Churches the faculty to establish sodalities and pious unions of the Blessed Sacrament instead of confraternities. Canon 549, §1, which deals with the order of precedence, however, lays down the principle that confraternities precede pious unions. Paragraph 2 of this canon employs the terminology, *confraternitas divinae Eucharistiae*, and grants to such a confraternity the right to precede all other confraternities. Nothing at all is said of the precedence of sodalities or pious unions of the Blessed Sacrament. Consistency seems to urge the conclusion that only confraternities of the Blessed Sacrament enjoy this right of precedence.

number of primary unions, or other ecclesiastical associations provided they are of the same kind and rank.[24]

The principle of peaceful quasi possession in canon 106, 5° reads in full: Among various moral persons of the same kind and rank, that one has precedence which is in peaceful quasi possession; if this cannot be determined, that one has precedence which was first established in the place of controversy. The latter principle of priority of establishment in a place applies only when quasi possession cannot be determined. It functions as a secondary and subsidiary norm.

These two canonical principles for establishing the right of precedence are drawn from the constitution *Exposcit* of Gregory XIII.[25] This constitution established the rules for precedence among ecclesiastical associations and remained in force as general pre-Code law. Since canon 106, 5° reenacts this legislation, it carries the same interpretation as the constitution carried prior to the Code of Canon Law.[26]

The primary source for determining the right of precedence among associations of the same kind and rank is peaceful quasi possession. The phrase *peaceful quasi possession* may be defined as the exercise of precedence for a period of time without a protest or a reservation of the right on the part of another. As soon as a formal protest is lodged or a controversy arises, the possession of precedence legally ceases to be peaceful. Even if the actual exercise of precedence is not legitimate in the objective order, as long as its use is not contested by another, the ecclesiastical association enjoys the peaceful quasi possession required by law. Authors state that the peaceful exercise of precedence must extend beyond a period of four or five years.[27] Accordingly, an archconfraternity which has exercised precedence among other archconfraternities uncontested for this length of time, enjoys the legal right to precedence.[28]

[24]Canons 701, §1, and 106, 5°.

[25]Gregory XIII, const. "*Exposcit,*" 15 iul. 1583—*Fontes*, n. 151.

[26]Canon 6, 2°. Cf. S. R. R., *Arequipa*, 4 maii 1926—*S. Romanae Rotae Decisiones seu Sententiae*, XVIII (1926), XX, 160.

[27]Cf. Matthaeus a Coronata, *Institutiones*, I, p. 191; Schreiber, P., *Canonical Precedence*, p. 195; Michiels, G., *De Personis*, p. 694; Regatillo, E., *Institutiones*, I, p. 173. A period of ten years is certainly sufficient to establish quasi possession. Cf. *S. R. R. Dec.*, XVIII (1926), XX, 162.

[28]Cf. S. R. R., *Arequipa*, 4 maii 1926—*S. R. R. Dec.*, XVIII (1926), XX, 161. In

It should be remarked here that the principle of peaceful quasi possession obtains only in cases dealing with associations of the same kind and rank. It does not apply in cases of precedence involving different ranks. For example, the principle may not be employed to determine precedence between an archconfraternity and a simple confraternity, or between a primary union and a pious union. These cases are subject exclusively to the norms found in canon 701.

The secondary or subsidiary source for determining precedence among ecclesiastical associations of the same kind and rank is that of priority of establishment in the place of controversy. This norm applies whenever quasi possession cannot be determined.[29] According to this rule, the association that can claim priority of foundation in the place where the controversy arises has the right to precede. This secondary norm is conditional in the sense that it becomes operative only if quasi possession is not established for any of the ecclesiastical associations involved in the dispute. It goes without saying that this principle may be invoked only on condition that the contending associations have been established in the place where the issue of precedence has been raised.

Strictly speaking, the term *locus* employed by the canon[30] refers to the material site of the dispute (e.g. the town or city), where the ecclesiastical associations have gathered to perform an ecclesiastical function. Still, there seems to be no doubt that the legislator's choice of the general term *locus* was meant to support a somewhat broader meaning. For instance, if there is question of a diocesan procession in the cathedral city, priority of establishment in the diocese is the deciding factor, not priority of establishment in the cathedral city. If the particular function is parochial in character, priority of establishment in the parish is the criterion for resolving the issue.[31] The character of the ecclesiastical function must be taken into account in order to determine the relevance and limits of this principle.

---

this decision the Sacred Rota explains in detail the practical application of the principle of quasi possession and the secondary principle of priority of time laid down in canon 106, 5°.

[29] Canon 106, 5°. Cf. Schreiber, P., *Canonical Precedence*, p. 195 ff.

[30] Canon 106, 5°. "Quae prius in *loco*, ubi quaestio oritur, instituta est; . . ."

[31] Cf. Larraona, A., *Commentarium pro Religiosis*, IV (1923), pp. 216-218; Michiels, G., *De Personis*, p. 695; Regatillo, E., *Institutiones*, I, p. 173; Schreiber, P., *Canonical Precedence*, p. 198.

In considering the norms for precedence discussed in this section, special attention must always be given to the types of associations subject to them. Canon 106, 5° considers only associations enjoying equal dignity and rank. In these cases one association cannot be preferred to another by reason of dominion or greater value, for the relevant norms presuppose equality in degree of excellence and dignity. The correct placement of such equal subjects is determined only by the legal principle: "Qui prior est tempore potior est iure."[32] The legislator has recourse to a general principle and applies it to the actual exercise of precedence. As a result of this procedure there emerges a primary norm: that association which peacefully enjoyed precedence prior to the controversy retains possession. The secondary, devolutory norm is also based on the principle: that association which is first in the order of establishment is first in the order of precedence. In effect, these two principles only reaffirm actual precedence. In the case where peaceful quasi possession is proven, the law prescribes that nothing be disturbed and the present order of precedence remain. When peaceful quasi possession cannot be proven, the association which enjoyed the place of honor when it existed alone continues in that condition despite the foundation of later associations. In both instances, the order of precedence is based upon considerations of a temporal character.

Section 3: *The Local Ordinary and Precedence Among Ecclesiastical Associations*

In the foregoing section two practical norms for determining precedence were considered. Both are sufficiently broad in scope to furnish a solution for most controversies. However, it has been the experience of the Holy See in the past to render individual decisions for cases in which the application of these principles is not at all clear.[33] To provide a definite and ready solution for complex cases, the Holy See by virtue of canon 106, 6° grants the local Ordinary legislative and judicial power over matters of precedence. His is the competency to establish the order of precedence among ecclesiastical associations in his diocese, either through episcopal or synodal legislation. In drafting appropriate

[32]Reg. 54, R. J., in VI°. Cf. Gregory XIII, const. *"Exposcit,"* 15 iul. 1583—*Fontes,* n. 151.

[33]Cf. the footnotes to canons 106, 491, 701.

norms, the local Ordinary must follow both the principles of canon law and the legitimate customs of the diocese, and give due consideration to the type of activities carried out by the various ecclesiastical associations within his territory.[34] Should a controversy arise and the case be urgent, the local Ordinary is empowered to settle the question by administrative decree. Urgent questions of precedence among primary societies are likewise subject to the local Ordinary's power. The mere fact that an association can be established as a primary association only by the Holy See does not exempt it from this discretionary power of the local Ordinary. Canon 701, §1 points out that all ecclesiastical associations are subject to the local Ordinary in urgent questions of precedence. Significantly, no exception is made to this rule.[35] Decisions given by the local Ordinary under these circumstances, it should be remembered, are not prejudicial to the inherent right of any association involved. His settlement of a controversy is transitory in character and applies only to the case in question. His verdict does not create a permanent right of precedence for the association in whose favor the decision is rendered. It merely provides a necessary solution for a case whose urgency does not allow a settlement by judicial process.[36] Ecclesiastical associations involved in such a dispute may have recourse against the decree of the local Ordinary. But such an appeal can only be *in devolutivo.* The reason for this is evident. Because the ecclesiastical function in question cannot be postponed, the controversy demands an immediate solution. A decision rendered under such circumstances must be definitive and continue in effect. If an appeal against such a decree had suspensive effect, there would be no competent authority to decide the order of precedence and the Holy See would hardly be within easy access of the litigants.[37]

[34]Canon 106, 6°. Cf. Schreiber, P., *Canonical Precedence,* p. 223 ff.

[35]Canon 701, §1. "Inter pias laicorum associationes, ordo praecedentiae est qui sequitur, firmo praescripto can. 106, nn. 5, 6: . . ."

[36]Canon 106, 6°. Cf. Michiels, G., *De Personis,* p. 696; Schreiber, P., *Canonical Precedence,* p. 237 ff.

[37]Canon 106, 6° gives the local Ordinary power to settle urgent cases of precedence even when various exempt religious are involved. This is only reasonable since some authority, in addition to the Holy See, should have the competency to settle matters of precedence in public functions and thereby ensure good order and proper decorum. Cf. Schreiber, P., *Canonical Precedence,* p. 237.

If a decision regarding precedence (when public order is concerned) is handed down by means of a regular process, the judge of the first instance, even for exempt religious, is the local Ordinary.[38] Appeal against the sentence of the court does not have suspensive effect.[39] An ecclesiastical association, wishing to have recourse against the decree of the local Ordinary, or to appeal a sentence relating to precedence, must direct its case to the Sacred Congregation of the Council.[40]

Section 4: Precedence Within an Archconfraternity or Primary Union

In the foregoing sections, the order of external precedence, or the proper ordering of one ecclesiastical association in relation to another, served as the focal point of discussion. This section deals with the internal precedence of an association, that is, the proper placement of the various members of an ecclesiastical society. Canon 106, 5° furnishes the norms which apply to the circumstances under consideration:

1) If the legitimate statutes of an association contain the order of precedence, these must be followed.

2) In the event the statutes do not have specific norms governing precedence, legitimate custom must determine it.

3) In the absence of legitimate custom, the prescriptions of common law are to be applied in determining the order of precedence.

The first rule for determining the order of precedence among the members of an ecclesiastical society is the statutory law of the association. If a definite order is prescribed in the statutes, it must be followed provided the statutes have been approved by competent authority. Should these statutory prescriptions be contrary to the regulations of common law, it seems certain that they must be followed if they have been legitimately approved. Canon 106, 5° could hardly have overlooked such a case in listing the sources which are to furnish the order of internal precedence. The legislator explicitly indicates that the prescriptions of common law are not to be applied if the approved statutes or

[38]Canon 1579, §3. If the question of precedence involves exempt religious of the same house, province, or order, the case would be handled according to the procedural rules of the religious institute. Cf. canon 1579, §1.

[39]Canon 106, 6°. Cf. Michiels, G., *De Personis*, p. 696.

[40]Canon 250, §3.

legitimate custom afford an order of precedence. The criterion of common law is subsidiary and is not meant to supplant either the norms of the particular statutes or legitimate custom. Furthermore, the fact that the legislator expressly singles out the common law as a subsidiary source, even though it is always implicitly understood to function in that capacity under similar circumstances, presupposes norms which may or may not be contrary to the common law.[41]

In the event the statutory law of an association does not provide specific norms of precedence, recourse is to be had to legitimate custom. Here the secondary and subsidiary source for the determination of internal precedence becomes operative. In case there are no legitimate customs in force, the general principles of precedence enunciated in the Code of Canon Law serve as the basis of procedure. For instance, clerics and religious who are members of an association would precede lay members.[42] The officials of the association precede mere members. Members who entered the association at an earlier date precede the more recently enrolled. Should two or more members have been enrolled at the same time, the older in age assumes the higher place of honor.[43] The practical application of these general principles of common law may at times present special difficulty. Consequently, each association should include in its statutes the order of dignity of its various offices, together with precise rules for determining precedence among its members. In this way, the proper order and decorum required by ecclesiastical services will be assured without controversy or conflict.[44]

[41]Cf. Michiels, G., *De Personis*, p. 692. Matthaeus a Coronata, *Institutiones*, I, p. 191, considers those statutes illegitimate which, even if approved, contain norms of precedence contrary to the principles of common law. However, a distinction seems in order at this point. Those statutes which had episcopal or apostolic approval prior to the Code may contain rules for precedence contrary to canonical principles. If so, these remain in force. After the Code of Canon Law, apostolically approved statutes which contain an order of precedence contrary to the prescriptions of the Code are likewise legitimate. However, after the Code, episcopal authority would not be sufficient to approve statutes containing prescriptions contrary to the Code, and therefore such statutes would be illegitimate. Cf. Vromant, G.-Bongaerts, L., *De Fidelium Associationibus*, p. 35; Schreiber, P., *Canonical Precedence*, p. 202 (footnote 8).

[42]Canons 119, 491.

[43]Cf. Canon 106, 3°; Matthaeus a Coronata, *Institutiones*, I, pp. 188 and 191.

[44]Cf. Schreiber, P., *Canonical Precedence*, p. 223.

Finally, the application of these canonical norms of internal precedence to an archconfraternity or primary union does not differ from their application in the case of any other ecclesiastical society. In the absence of particular statutes and legitimate custom, the general canonical principles are to be applied in the manner described in the preceding paragraphs. The supreme moderator and chaplain of the primary society will take the higher places of honor among the members. In ecclesiastical functions where the chaplain exercises his office, he should have the highest place of honor. At all other times the supreme moderator retains the highest place of honor by reason of his supreme office. The president and officers of the primary society follow next in the order of precedence. After them follow the rest of the members in the order of their enrollment, or should enrollment not be a decisive criterion, physical age.[45]

Section 5: *Conditions Required to Exercise the Right of Precedence*

Archconfraternities and primary unions, as well as other associations enjoying the right of precedence, must fulfill certain conditions in order to exercise this right. Since the formal and specific significance of this privilege arises from and is conditioned by the activity of the society as a collective entity, its exercise is warranted only when the society is represented through group activity. Therefore, in ecclesiastical functions such as processions or in public conventions, an association may exercise the right of precedence only if it is properly represented by a group of its members. Canon 701, §3 requires collegiate presence of the association as a condition for the exercise of its right of precedence. Accordingly, at least three members of the society would have to be grouped together to be considered official representatives.[46]

Furthermore canonical measures prescribe that this representative group of members appear with the cross or banner of the association and that the members wear the distinctive garb or the insignia proper to their society. These provisions ensure the necessary identification of each association and help to maintain the order of precedence once

[45]If there are cleric or religious members in the association, they precede even a lay president in accordance with the general principle of canon 491.

[46]Canon 701, §3. "Omnes autem tunc solummodo ius praecedentiae habent, cum collegialiter incedunt sub propria cruce vel vexillo et cum habitu seu insignibus associationis."

established.[47] The garb or insignia must be proper to the association so as to fulfill its specific purpose, namely, to distinguish its members from the members of other associations. The same applies in the case of the banner or standard. In most instances, if the banner contains the official title of the association and the church or town in which it is situated, it will readily identify the association and distinguish it from any other.[48]

47Canon 701, §3 reads "...cum habitu *seu* insignibus associationis." *Seu* in this canon is disjunctive in meaning. Therefore a collegiate body of members wearing the proper insignia of their association (e.g., scapular or medal) enjoy the right of precedence even if not dressed in their distinctive habit. The Code itself makes a distinction between the habit and the insignia (cf. canons 703, 706, 713, §2, 714, 718), and canon 701, §3 seems to allow the use of either one. Cf. Matthaeus a Coronata, *Institutiones,* I, pp. 909-910. With regard to the Third Order of St. Francis, however, consult the private response of the S. C. of Religious, March 30, 1925, found in the *Canon Law Digest,* III, p. 292.

48Cf. Matthaeus a Coronata, *Institutiones,* I, p. 910. For an excellent treatment of the law prior to the Code of Canon Law, cf. A. Tachy, *Traité des Confréries,* pp. 195-221.

SUPPLEMENT

CHAPTER VII

THE ARCHCONFRATERNITY OF CHRISTIAN MOTHERS

Article 1: Origin and History

The first association of Christian Mothers originated at Lille, France, on May 1, 1850. On this date a large group of mothers gathered to exchange views on the various problems involved in the education and training of their children. The convention placed itself under the patronage of the Immaculate Virgin, the Mother of Sorrows. The inspiration and organizing force behind the movement found concrete expression in the person of Madame Jossen de Bilhem, who was appointed the president of the first association. Through the untiring efforts of Father Theodore Ratisbonne the organization soon spread to a number of parishes in and around Paris. In 1856, he petitioned Pope Pius IX to raise the association established in Paris, in the chapel of the religious of Notre Dame de Sion, to the rank of a primary society. On March 11, 1856, the Holy Father graciously acceded to the request, conferring upon the society the power to affiliate all other societies of the same title and purpose.[1] Father Ratisbonne became the first Director General of the primary association in Paris.

Before long, the association had spread throughout France,[2] and into Germany and Austria. By 1871 the number of societies in Germany had grown impressively. At the request of the Bishop of Regensburg, the association established in the Church of St. Giles was elevated to the rank of primary association, by Pope Pius IX, on December 12, 1871.[3]

[1]This material has been gathered from a number of sources. One may consult the *Dictionnarie Practique des Connaissances Religieuses* (Paris: Librairie Letouzey et Ané, 1926), *Mères Chrétiennes*, cols. 898-900; Beringer, F.-Steinen, P., *Die Ablaesse*, II, n. 309; Seraphinus de Angelis, *De Fidelium Associationibus*, II, p. 109.

[2]By 1922 there were 2800 canonically established associations with 2 million members in France alone. These were affiliated to the primary association established in Notre Dame de Sion Chapel, in Paris. The address of the central office of this association is: 61, Rue Notre Dame des Champs, Paris.

[3]The address of the Director General of this primary society is: Niedermunstergasse 1, Regensburg, Germany.

By virtue of apostolic brief the affiliation between the primary association in Paris and the association in Regensburg was dissolved. The latter was raised to the rank of primary society and given the power to affiliate within the German Empire and in the neighboring countries where the faithful spoke the German language.[4] At this writing the Regensburg Association has affiliated 346 local associations within the diocese and 6,930 others spread throughout Germany, and in parts of Austria and Switzerland.[5]

The Capuchin Friars, who were acquainted with the associations in Germany, were instrumental in organizing Societies of Christian Mothers in various parts of the United States. In the year 1877, the Most Reverend John Tuigg, Bishop of Pittsburgh, established an association at the Capuchin Church of St. Augustine in the city of Pittsburgh. At the request of the Very Rev. Francis Xavier, Minister Provincial of the Capuchin Province of Bavaria, Pope Leo XIII raised the association of Christian Mothers established at that church to the rank of primary association and granted it the power to affiliate.[6] Under the influence and direction of the Capuchin Order, the association spread rapidly through the United States. Currently, more than 2,800 associations have been established in the United States. In this country there is only one primary society, that of the association established in St. Augustine's Church in Pittsburgh. Requests for affiliation to this association should be directed to the Moderator of the primary association who is empowered to issue the decree of affiliation.[7]

[4]Cf. Beringer F.-Steinen, P., *Die Ablaesse,* II, n. 309. Much of the factual data on the Regensburg Association was made available to the writer by personal communication, under date of Jan. 10, 1959, from the Director General of the association. Opportunity is here taken to express sincerest thanks to him.

[5]The Most Reverend William Emmanuel Ketteler, Bishop of Mainz, may justly be called the founder and promoter of the associations of Christian Mothers in Germany. He introduced the association into his diocese as early as 1860. However, upon the request of Bishop Ignatius von Senestréy of Regensburg, at a later date, the association established in Regensburg in St. Giles's Church, was elevated to the rank of primary society and granted the power to affiliate.

[6]Cf. the appendix for the pertinent documents. The original rescripts are preserved in the archives of the Archconfraternity of Christian Mothers, 220—37th Street, Pittsburgh 1, Pa. Also cf. the *Analecta Capuccinorum,* VIII, p. 103.

[7]The present Moderator is Father Bertin Roll, O.F.M. Cap., who has set up a central information office on the association of Christian Mothers and makes the

ARTICLE 2: TITLE AND PURPOSE

The official title of the different associations of Christian Mothers, according to various papal documents, must contain the designation "Christian Mothers."[8] This phrase is singularly expressive of the character of the association and forms an essential element of the official title of each association seeking affiliation to the primary society. In this regard, it does not seem necessary for an association seeking affiliation to have the same principal patroness as the primary society, even though a doubt concerning this point may arise from the wording of various documents from the Holy See. For example, the first brief of indulgences to the association of Christian Mothers in Paris bore the title, *"Pia sodalitas sub titulo 'Les Mères Chrétiennes' ac sub invocatione B.M.V. Septem Dolorum canonice erecta."* The association at Ratisbonne, in a grant of indulgences, was designated as *"Pia quaedam mulierum fidelium sodalitas sub titulo—Matrum Christianarum—et invocatione Beatae Virginis Perdolentis."* And when the latter association was raised to the rank of primary union, the proper designation was: "Sodality of Christian Mothers under the patronage and protection *'Beatissimae Mariae Virginis et Matris Perdolentis'* " and it is permitted to affiliate associations *"eiusdem invocationis et instituti."*[9]

However, the association canonically established at St. Augustine's Church in Pittsburgh has as its official title, "Christian Mothers." Although it too is placed under the patronage and protection of the *Sorrowful Mother,* the document raising the association to the rank of primary union simply used the title, "Christian Mothers." No mention of the patronage of the Blessed Virgin Mary was made in the official

copious literature of the association available to its affiliates and other interested parties. At present there are three other primary associations of Christian Mothers besides those already mentioned. The association established in the Church of San Agostino, Rome, was raised to the status of primary association in 1863; the society at St. Barbara's Church, Cracow, was similarly honored in 1913; and recently, in 1944, the association of Christian Mothers set up in the Abbatial Church of the Order of St. Benedict in Einsiedeln, Switzerland, was raised to the rank of Primary Union by Pius XII. Cf. *AAS,* XXXVII (1945), 108-110; Beringer, F.-Steinen, P., *Die Ablaesse,* II, n. 309.

[8]Cf. Appendix.

[9]Cf. Beringer, F.-Steinen, P., *Die Ablaesse,* II, n. 309.

title, as in the case of the primary society of Regensburg.[10] Nor can an argument be advanced from the reply of the Sacred Congregation of Indulgences, July 17, 1891,[11] which dealt with two different associations, both bearing the title *Bona Mors*. In this case the complete official title of the primary society was *"Congregatio sub invocatione D.N. Jesu Christi in Cruce morientis et B.M.V. perdolentis,"* while the title of the society seeking affiliation read *Bona Mors sub invocatione Sancti Josephi.*[12] In this case it is evident that the association seeking affiliation did not have the same title as the primary society. Besides, the specific purpose of each association was different and therefore the two could not in any way be considered to have the *same title and purpose*, a condition necessary for valid affiliation.[13]

In view of the terminology of the rescript elevating the Association of Christian Mothers established at St. Augustine's Church to the rank of primary union, one may rightly argue that the complete official title consists in the designation "Christian Mothers." In confirmation of this interpretation one may cite the recent apostolic letter of Pius XII which created a primary union of Christian Mothers in Einsiedeln, Switzerland. In this document the Roman Pontiff raised the Pious Union of Christian Mothers, canonically established in the Abbatial Church in Einsiedeln, to the rank of primary union. The association is under the patronage of the Blessed Virgin Mary of Einsiedeln and Saint Meinrad. However, the complete official title is the "Primary Union of Christian Mothers."[14] Other associations, provided they bear the official title

[10]Beringer, F.-Steinen, P., argue that the invocation, "Beatissimae Mariae Virginis et Matris Perdolentis," is part of the official title of the Ratisbon primary society and therefore all affiliates must make mention of it in their official titles.—Beringer, F.-Steinen, P., *Die Ablaesse,* II, n. 309.

[11]S. C. Indulg., *Albien.,* 17 iul. 1891—*Fontes,* n. 5112.

[12]Benedict XIII, const. *"Redemptoris nostri,"* 21 sept. 1729—*Bull. Rom. Taur.,* XXII, p. 843: "...congregationem sub invocatione domini nostri Jesu Christi in cruce moribundi ac Beatissimae Virginis Mariae eius genitricis dolorosae, vulgo *della Buona Morte* nuncupatam..."

[13]S. C. Indulg., *Albien.,* 17 iul. 1891—*Fontes,* n. 5112.

[14]Pius XII, litt. apost., 19 mart. 1944—*AAS,* XXXVII (1945), 109: "...Apostolica Nostra auctoritate, perpetuumque in modum, *Piam Unionem Matrum Christianarum,* vulgo 'Bruderschaft Christlicher Muetter' nuncupatam,...ad *Primariae* dignitatem evehimus."

"Christian Mothers" and have the same purpose, may be affiliated to this primary union.

The same is to be said of the Primary Union of Christian Mothers canonically established in the Church of St. Augustine in Pittsburgh. The text of the rescript which raised the association to the status of primary union placed the complete title in the term "Christian Mothers."[15] Furthermore, in an earlier rescript which granted a number of indulgences to the association, Pope Leo XIII explicitly referred to the association by the title of "Christian Mothers."[16] In view of this cumulative evidence there is no doubt that the complete official title of the Primary Union established in the Church of St. Augustine is "Christian Mothers." Consequently, an association seeking affiliation must have the title "Christian Mothers" and be committed to the same purpose. It is not necessary to have the same patron or patrons to achieve affiliation.[17]

The specific purpose of associations of Christian Mothers is the Catholic education of children by their mothers. Any other religious activity engaged in by a Christian Mother society is supplementary and cannot be regarded as the proper aim. The purpose and goal of each of these associations must be the thoroughly Catholic education of the child. For this reason, valid affiliation with the Primary Union of Christian Mothers of St. Augustine's Church, Pittsburgh, requires that the affiliate have as its title "Christian Mothers," and for its specific object, the Catholic education of children by their mothers.[18]

[15]"...sub titulo Matrum Christianarum canonice erectam..." Cf. Appendix, p. 124.

[16]"Cum, sicut accepimus, in Parochiali S. Augustini Ecclesia civitatis Pittsburgensis pia mulierum Christifidelium Sodalitas Matrum Christianarum titulo canonice instituta sit..." Cf. Appendix, p. 124.

[17]The director's and officer's manual for the establishment and direction of the association of Christian Mothers accepts the opposite opinion. However, in view of pre-Code as well as present legislation the opinion lacks juridical foundation. Nowhere is it required for an affiliate to have the same patron as a condition for valid affiliation. Cf. canons 720-723.

[18]Cf. Appendix, p. 128.

Article 3: Juridical Nature of the Archconfraternity of Christian Mothers

The Primary Association of Christian Mothers canonically established in St. Augustine's Church, Pittsburgh, Pa., is popularly known as the "Archconfraternity of Christian Mothers." This term *archconfraternity* used as a component in the designation of the Christian Mothers association is juridically incorrect. Strictly speaking, the Code of Canon Law defines *confraternity* as an association that has for its purpose the promotion of public worship and has the organizational features of a corporate society. By definition, an *archconfraternity* is a confraternity which has been raised to the rank of primary society.[19] The Primary Association of Christian Mothers does not have for its specific purpose the promotion of public worship. Therefore it is not properly speaking an archconfraternity. It is to be identified rather as a type of pious union, defined in canon 707, §1. The "Archconfraternity of Christian Mothers" is in reality a primary union of Christian Mothers.[20]

The question arises whether the association of Christian Mothers is, in canonical language, a *sodality*. According to the definition of the Code of Canon Law, a sodality is a pious union that has an internal hierarchical organization with president, councilors, administrators, and other officers. This internal government is structured after the manner of an organic body in which the members enjoy the right to hold formal meetings, issue special norms affecting the association, elect officers who direct the work of the association and administer the common holdings.[21] The whole internal organization of the sodality forms an organic body with its president and officers holding elective offices.

Now, in the general statutes of the Primary Association of Christian Mothers, statute No. IX explicitly states that the director (who is appointed by the Bishop) is to name the president and vice-president of the association.[22] The special statutes approved for the Primary Asso-

[19]Canons 707, §2 and 720.

[20]This was the technical designation used by Pius XII in elevating the Pious Union of Christian Mothers in Einsiedeln to the rank of Primary Union. Cf. *AAS*, XXXVII (1945), 109.

[21]Canons 707, §1 and 697, §1.

[22]IX. The Director of the whole confraternity is the Director appointed by the Bishop. The Director will appoint the lady President and the lady Vice-President for a term of three years. To direct and manage larger confraternities the better,

ciation at St. Augustine's Church also contains a provision that places the power of appointing officers in the director.[23] In view of these regulations, the Primary Association at St. Augustine's may not be considered an archsodality in the canonical sense. It answers rather to the canonical description of a primary union. Even though the association does have a limited organization among its members, it does not possess the elements essential to the corporate structure demanded of a sodality. In view of this, the "Archconfraternity of Christian Mothers" established at St. Augustine's Church, Pittsburgh, juridically speaking, possesses the true and proper nature of a primary union.[24]

Article 4: The Extent of the Power of Affiliation

On January 16, 1881, Pope Leo XIII raised the association of Christian Mothers canonically established in St. Augustine's Church to the rank of primary union. At the same time he granted it the power to affiliate other associations of the same title and purpose already established or to be established in the diocese of Pittsburgh or other dioceses.[25] When treating of the extent of this power to affiliate, Beringer restricts the faculty of affiliation to the diocese of Pittsburgh and to other dioceses of North America.[26] Seeberger would limit the faculty only to associations established in the United States.[27]

---

they are divided into sections presided over by a lady Prefect and a lady Assistant Prefect. They are also to be appointed by the Director, and to be changed from time to time at his discretion.—*Manual for Directors and Officers,* (6. ed., Pittsburgh: Archconfraternity of Christian Mothers, 1957), p. 47.

[23]*Ibidem,* p. 55.

[24]Pius XII, in raising the "Bruderschaft Christlicher Muetter" in Einsiedeln, Switzerland, to the status of primary society, employed canonically correct terminology, *primary union.* "... *piam unionem Matrum Christianarum,* vulgo 'Bruderschaft Christlicher Muetter' nuncupatam, ... ad *Primariae* dignitatem evehimus; ipsiusque Primariae Unionis nunc per Nos erectae ..."—*AAS,* XXXVII (1945), 109.

[25]The exact text of the document reads: "... elevando nempe eamdem Sodalitatem ad gradum Archisodalitatis, ita ut in posterum Director possit et valeat alias Sodalitates, sub eodem titulo in Pittsburgensi aut aliis in Diocesibus institutas aut instituendas, aggregare, ..."—*Appendix,* p. 124.

[26]Beringer, F.-Steinen, P., *Die Ablaesse,* II, n. 309.

[27]Seeberger, M., *Key to the Spiritual Treasures,* p. 271.

However, the text of the document can hardly be construed as support for their opinions. The canonical principles basic to the interpretation of rescripts granting favors must be applied in this case. Prior to the Code of Canon Law at the time of the issuance of the rescript, the principle to be applied for the correct interpretation of rescripts was the same as that enunciated in canon 49. The principle is this: rescripts are to be understood according to the proper meaning of the words and common usage, and are not to be extended to cases other than those expressed in them.[28]

The precise wording of the indult reads: "...in posterum Director possit et valeat alias Sodalitates, sub eodem titulo in Pittsburgensi aut aliis in Diocesibus institutas aut instituendas aggregare..." According to the proper meaning then, the power to affiliate may be exercised in the diocese of Pittsburgh and in other dioceses. The words "aliis diocesibus" are general terms and are to be understood in that manner. To restrict the meaning of this phrase to "dioceses of the United States" or even "dioceses of the North American Continent" is to modify the meaning and thereby to limit the comprehension of the text. Consequently, the opinions of Beringer[29] and Seeberger[30] lack juridical foundation, for both are based on an incorrect interpretation of the indult.

According to the proper interpretation of the indult, the faculty to affiliate granted to the Primary Union of Christian Mothers in St. Augustine's Church, Pittsburgh, is universal. It extends to dioceses all over the world. It is not limited to a certain territory nor to a certain language group.[31] As a matter of fact, the faculty is limitless in its extension because it was not expressly restricted. Consequently, the Primary Union of Christian Mothers established in St. Augustine's Church, Pittsburgh, Pa., may affiliate similar Christian Mother societies situated

[28]Canon 67 reads: a privilege is to be understood according to its wording, and may not be extended or restricted. Cf. Reiffenstuel, A., *Ius Canonicum Universum,* lib. I, tit. 3, n. 119; Schmalzgrueber, F., *Ius Ecclesiasticum Universum,* lib. I, tit. 3, n. 24 ff.

[29]*Die Ablaesse,* II, n. 309.

[30]*Key to the Spiritual Treasures,* p. 271.

[31]The Primary Union of Christian Mothers established in Einsiedeln, Switzerland, enjoys a limited faculty to affiliate. Cf. *AAS,* XXXVII (1945), 109.

in any diocese in the world—even in those dioceses where other primary societies of Christian Mothers exist.[32]

[32]This interpretation is confirmed by the pre-Code practice of the Holy See in the granting of faculties of affiliation. If no restriction was expressly stated in the indult, the faculty to affiliate was considered to be of universal extent. Cf. S. C. Indulg., *Firmana,* 20 iul. 1868—*ASS,* IV (1868-1869), 271. Cf. also p. 54 of this dissertation.

CONCLUSIONS

1. The elevation of ecclesiastical societies to the status of primary societies became a common phenomenon in the 16th century. The Roman Pontiffs always reserved to themselves the right to confer on an ecclesiastical society the title of primary status together with the power to affiliate similar societies and communicate to them its privileges and indulgences.

2. The *Quaecumque* of Clement VIII (1592-1605) was the most important and comprehensive piece of legislation dealing with primary societies to the publication of the Code of Canon Law. Although it has lost its juridic force as common law, the *Quaecumque* retains importance as the main interpretative source for canons 720-725.

3. The establishment, transfer, and suppression of archconfraternities and primary unions are reserved exclusively to the Holy See.

4. The difference between an archconfraternity and a confraternity, an archsodality and a sodality, a primary union and a pious union, is one of degree not of kind. The rank of primary status adds only an accidental difference to the original nature of the society.

5. The power to affiliate granted to primary societies includes an automatic communication of their privileges and indulgences which were granted to the primary societies directly and specifically by the Holy See. After affiliation, future grants of apostolic privileges and indulgences to the primary societies are communicated *ipso iure* to the affiliates.

6. The supreme moderator of the primary society cannot delegate the power to affiliate unless this fact is expressly mentioned in the apostolic indult.

7. Primary societies possess the faculty to affiliate similar ecclesiastical societies, that is, societies bearing the same official title and pursuing the same purpose. The statutory laws of the affiliates need not conform to those of the primary society, nor need they be established in honor of the same patron as the affiliating society.

8. According to the common opinion, a society seeking affiliation must, as a valid condition for affiliation, possess moral personality. However, an opposite probable opinion maintains that an ecclesiastically approved society (one lacking moral personality) can validly and licitly request and receive affiliation with a primary society.

9. On the occasion of an affiliation, the primary society may not receive a donation or an offering from the affiliate. Nor may the primary society accept an alms from the affiliate which would be applied to its specific work. A monetary recompense to cover the necessary expenses of affiliation is not forbidden.

10. The communication of indulgences and spiritual privileges effected through affiliation follows the accessory form of communication. Affiliated societies always remain in the position of accessories with respect to grants made to the primary society. However, indulgences and privileges possessed by the affiliated society prior to its affiliation remain intact and unaffected.

11. The grant of indulgences, privileges, and other spiritual favors to primary societies from the Holy See is subject only to such limitations as are expressly stated in the apostolic indult. In the absence of any restrictive clause, these grants must be considered absolute and perpetual.

12. Archconfraternities precede confraternities and primary unions precede pious unions since primary societies are of a different rank. Precedence within a primary society is determined by statutory law; in the absence of specific statutes, custom is the determining factor. And in the event that neither statutory law nor custom is a decisive norm, the general principles of canon law are to be applied.

13. The *Archconfraternity of Christian Mothers* (located in St. Augustine's Church, Pittsburgh, Pa.) is, canonically, a primary union.

14. The *Archconfraternity of Christian Mothers* possesses an unrestricted faculty to affiliate similar ecclesiastical associations established anywhere in the world.

APPENDIX

I. Elevation of the Association of Christian Mothers (Church of St. Augustine, Pittsburgh, Pa.) to the Status of Primary Union.

The elevation of the Association of Christian Mothers (Church of St. Augustine, Pittsburgh, Pa.) to the status of primary union with the faculty of affiliation, was effected by virtue of the following document:

Beatissime Pater. Fr. Franciscus Xaverius ab Ilmimonasterio, Provinciae Capucinorum Bavariae Minister, ad pedes S.V. humiliter provolutus, exponit, quod piam mulierum Sodalitatem in Ecclesia parochiali S. Augustini Ordinis Capucinorum Civitatis Pittsburgensis sub titulo Matrum Christianarum canonice erectam plurimis indulgentiis sive plenariis, sive partialibus S.V. per Breve diei 7 Maii 1878 ditare dignata est.

Orator nunc humillime supplicat, quatenus praedictam Sodalitatem novo favore Sanctitas Vestra pro sua benignitate insignire velit, elevando nempe eamdem Sodalitatem ad gradum Archisodalitatis, ita ut in posterum Director possit et valeat alias Sodalitates, sub eodem titulo in Pittsburgensi aut aliis in Dioecesibus institutas aut instituendas, aggregare, ea tamen lege, ut Sodalitas in altera Dioecesi canonice erecta aggregari nequeat, nisi obtentis in hunc finem respectivi Ordinarii approbatione et commendatione.

Ad quod rescriptum fuit:

Ex Audientia SSmi diei 16 Ianuarii 1881.

SSmus Dominus Noster Leo, Divina Providentia PP. XIII . . . referente me infrascripto S. Congnis. de Propaganda Fide Secretario, porrectis precibus benigne in omnibus annuere dignatus est pro gratia iuxta petita, servatis servandis.

Datum Romae ex Aed. S. Congnis. die et anno ut supra.
Fr. Mascotti Secrius.

Executioni hisce demandatur. Datum apud Pittsburgensem.
Die 3 Martii, 1881.
†J. Tuigg
Epus. Pittsburgensis
et Admin. Alleghenensis.
Gratis quocumque titulo

II. Texts of Papal Grants of Indulgences

Papal Concessions of Indulgences to the Sodality of Christian Mothers established in the Church of Saint Augustine, Pittsburgh, Pa.

1. Papal Brief of May 7, 1878.

Leo PP. XIII.

Ad perpetuam rei memoriam. Cum, sicut accepimus, in Parochiali S. Augustini

Ecclesia civitatis Pittsburgensis pia mulierum Christifidelium Sodalitas Matrum Christianarum titulo canonice instituta sit, cujus Sodales plurima pietatis et charitatis opera exercere consueverunt; Nos, ut Sodalitas huiusmodi maiora in dies suscipiat incrementa, de Omnipotentis Dei misericordia ac BB. Petri et Pauli App. eius auctoritate confisi, omnibus mulieribus Christifidelibus, quae dictam Sodalitatem in posterum ingredientur, die primo earum ingressus, si vere poenitentes et confessae Sanctissimum Eucharistiae Sacramentum sumpserint, plenariam; ac tam descriptis, quam pro tempore describendis in dicta Sodalitate Consororibus in cuiuslibet earum mortis articulo, si vere quoque poenitentes et confessae ac S. Communione refectae, vel quatenus id facere nequiverint, saltem contritae Nomen Iesu, ore si potuerint, sin minus corde, devote invocaverint, etiam plenariam; necnon eisdem nunc et pro tempore existentibus in dicta Sodalitate Consororibus, vere etiam poenitentibus et confessis ac S. Communione refectis, quae praefatae Sodalitatis Ecclesiam seu Cappellam vel Oratorium die festo principali dictae Sodalitatis, per easdem Consorores semel tantum eligendo et ab Ordinario approbando, vel uno ex septem diebus continuis immediate subsequentibus, singulis annis devote visitaverint, et ibi pro Christianorum Principum concordia, haeresum extirpatione, peccatorum conversione ac S. Matris Ecclesiae exaltatione pias ad Deum preces effuderint, plenariam similiter omnium peccatorum suorum Indulgentiam et remissionem misericorditer in Domino concedimus. Praeterea memoratis Consororibus, corde saltem contritis Ecclesiam seu Capellam vel Oratorium huiusmodi in quatuor aliis anni feriatis vel non feriatis seu Dominicis diebus, per memoratas Consorores semel tantum eligendis et ab eodem Ordinario approbandis, ut supra visitantibus et ibidem orantibus, quo die praefatorum id egerint, septem annos ac totidem quadragenas; quoties vero bonum aliquod opus iuxta Sodalitatis ipsius institutum in Domino peregerint, toties sexaginta dies de iniunctis eis, seu alias quomodolibet debitis poenitentiis in forma Ecclesiae consueta relaxamus. Quas omnes et singulas Indulgentias, peccatorum remissiones ac poenitentiarum relaxationes etiam animabus Christifidelium, quae Deo in charitate coniunctae ab hac luce migraverint, per modum suffragii applicari posse indulgemus. In contrarium facientibus non obstantibus quibuscumque. Praesentibus perpetuis futuris temporibus valituris. Volumus autem, ut, si alias dictis Consororibus praemissa peragentibus aliqua alia Indulgentia similis perpetuo vel ad tempus nondum elapsum duratura concessa fuerit, illa revocata sit, prout per praesentes Apostolica Nostra Auctoritate revocamus; atque, si dicta Sodalitas alicui Archisodalitati aggregata iam sit, vel in posterum aggregetur, aut quavis alia ratione uniatur, vel etiam quomodolibet instituatur, priores et quaevis aliae Litterae Apostolicae illis nullatenus suffragentur, sed ex tunc eo ipso nullae sint.

Datum Romae apud S. Petrum sub Annulo Piscatoris die VII.
Maii MDCCCLXXVIII. Pontificatus Nostri anno primo.

Pro Domino Card. Asquinio
L.S. D. Jacobini Subst.
Executioni hisce demandatur.

†J. Tuigg
Epus Pittsburgensis et
Admin. Alleghenensis
Pittsburgii die 30 Octobris, 1878.

Executioni hisce demandatur.
Vetoetlingae die, XVII Maii, 1878.
P. Franciscus Xaverius, Provinc. Capucin. Bavarii
p.t. Minister Provincialis.

2. Rescript of July 20, 1884.

Ex. P. Hyacinthus a Durachio, Ord. Min. Capucinorum Provinciae Pennsilvanicae Moderator, ad pedes Sanctitatis Vestrae humillime provolutus, exponit, qualiter benignitas Apostolica Sodalitati Matrum Christianarum, in Ecclesia Fr. Min. Capucinorum civitatis Pittsburgensis rite erectae, varias indulgentias concesserit. Nunc autem ad Matrum Christianarum, incitandum zelum et bonum magis ac magis promovendum humilis Exponens pro Consororibus, quae vere poenitentes et confessae ac sacra Communione refectae Ecclesiam respectivae Sodalitatis vel aliam visitaverint ibique pias ad Deum preces effuderint, indulgentiam plenariam enixe implorat:

In festivitatibus Epiphaniae D.N.J.C., Imm. Conceptionis et Purificationis B. Mariae Virginis, — in diebus festis S. Joseph Sponsi et S. Annae, genitricis eiusdem B.M.V., S. Augustini E.C.D., Ecclesiae Sodalitatis Patroni, S. Antonii a Patavio, S. Monicae, in festo Septem Dolorum B.M.V., SS. Angelorum Custodum, necnon in Commemoratione Omnium Fidelium Defunctorum, quas omnes indulgentias esse defunctis applicabiles Sanctitas Vestra concedere dignetur.

Et rescriptum est:

Ex Audientia SSmi diei 20 Iulii 1884.

SSmus Dominus Noster Leo, Divina Providentia PP. XIII, referente me infrascripto S. Congnis. de Propaganda Fide Secretario, plenariam indulgentiam in perpetuum animabus quoque in Purgatorio detentis applicabilem per modum suffragii benigne concedere dignatus est, ab omnibus et singulis, de quibus in precibus, lucrandam, sequentibus diebus festis tantum, nempe: Immaculatae Conceptionis Beatae Mariae Virginis, Epiphaniae D.N.J.C., et S. Joseph C., Sponsi B.M.V., dummodo vere poenitentes et confessae ac sacra Communione refectae Ecclesiam respectivae Sodalitatis vel aliam visitaverint ibique aliquas pias preces pro sanctae fidei propagatione et iuxta Summi Pontificis intentionem effuderint.

Datum Romae ex Aed. dictae S. Congnis. die et anno praedictis.

Gratis quocumque titulo

Pro R.P.D. Secretario
Ant. Agliardi off.

3. Rescript of March 28, 1886.

Beatissime Pater. P. Fr. Gregorius a Moguntia O.M. Cap. Provinciae S. Augustini Pennsilvanicae Archisodalitatis Matrum Christianarum Pittsburgensis Director Generalis, ad pedes S.V. humillime provolutus, exponit, qualiter memoratam Sodalitatem, canonice erectam in Ecclesia Parochiali S. Augustini Conventus Min. Cap., civitatis ac Dioecesis Pittsburgensis in America Septentrionali, aliquibus indulgentiis ditare eamque per Rescriptum S. C. de Propaganda Fide, die 16 Ianuarii 1881, emanatum ad gradum Archisodalitatis rite elevare cum solitis iuribus ac privilegiis S. V. benigne dignata fuerit.

Porro multiplicatis aggregationibus membrisque Sodalitatum, quum plures associationes huius instituti nonnullis in urbibus aut locis propinquis — in diversis quidem Parochiis, sed eadem lingua utentibus — vel existant vel praeparentur; in dies magis sentiuntur commoda, quae proventura essent tum lege distantiae sublata, tum indulgentiis propositis:

Quibus de causis humilis Orator supplicat:

1. S. V. dictae Archisodalitati concedere dignetur singulas indulgentias plenarias, animabus quoque purgatorio detentis applicabiles his quatuor diebus festis: Septem Dolorum B.M.V., mense Septembris celebrari solito, S. Annae, Monicae, SS. Angelorum Custodum, vel uno ex septem diebus immediate subsequentibus lucrandas, modo fideles, vere poenitentes ac confessae et S. Communione refectae, aliquam Ecclesiam visitaverint atque ad mentem S. V. oraverint.

2. S. V. dignetur dictam Archisodalitatem Sodalitatesque Matrum Christianarum, in America Septentrionali erigendas atque eidem aggregandas, solvere a lege distantiae.

3. S. V. declarare dignetur, conditionem visitandi ecclesiam Sodalitatis, aliquibus indulgentiarum concessionibus adiectam, non obstare, quin adscribantur absentes. Et Deus......

Tulit responsum:

Ex Audientia SSmi habita die 28 Martii 1886.

SSmus Dominus Noster Leo. Divina Providentia PP. XIII, referente me infrascripto S. Congnis. de Propaganda Fide Secretario, quo magis ac magis in dies augeatur pietas Christifidelium Matrum memoratae Archisodalitati adscriptarum eisque aliae ad S. Religionis incrementum in posterum adnumerentur; sequentes novas indulgentias ac privilegia favore earumdem iam alias concessis adiungere benigne dignatus est in perpetuum.

1. Plenariam peccatorum indulgentiam, applicabilem quoque per modum suffragii animabus in purgatorio detentis favore adscriptarum concessit, lucrandam festis diebus S. Annae, B. Mariae Virginis Matris, et S. Monicae, dummodo supra dictae Christifideles mulieres, vere poenitentes, confessae ac sacra Communione refectae, Ecclesiam seu Oratorium Archisodalitatis vel propriam parochialem devote visitaverint, ibique aliquas pias preces pro sanctae Fidei propagatione et iuxta Summi Pontificis intentionem effuderint.

2. Praefatam autem Archisodalitatem et Sodalitates sub eiusdem titulo ac dependentia erectas, sive in posterum erigendas, a lege distantiae exemptas declaravit.

3. Indulsit insuper Sanctitas Sua, ut omnes et singulae Indulgentiae, sive per praesens Rescriptum, sive aliter in antecessum Archisodalitati eidem concessae sub conditione Ecclesiam seu Capellam vel Oratorium Archisodalitatis ipsius visitandi, pari modo lucrari valeant visitata Ecclesia uniuscuiusque adscriptae propria, servatis

tamen in reliquo omnibus, quae in respectivis concessionibus praescribuntur.

Datum Romae ex Aed. dictae S. Congnis. die et anno ut supra.

D. Archiep. Tyren. Secr.

Promulgari permittitur.
Pittsburgii, die 22 Iunii, 1886.
De Mandato Illmi. ac Rmi. Epi.
†R. Phelan, V.G.
Coadj. Episc. Pittsb.
Gratis quocumque titulo

4. Rescript of February 17, 1889.

Beatissime Pater,

P. Gregorius a Moguntia Ord. Minor. Capuc. Director Generalis Archisodalitatis Matrum Christianarum Pittsburgii in America Septentrionali ad pedes S. V. humiliter provolutus, exponit ut sequitur.

Ad hanc S. Augustini D. E. ecclesiam existit sodalitas titulo Matrum Christianarum sub patrocinio B. Mariae Virginis ac Matris Perdolentis canonice erecta, quae pro fine principali habet promotionem et emendationem domesticae educationis per matres familiarum vere Christianas. Cui Sodalitati S. V. die 7 Maii 1878, dignata est elargiri complures indulgentias, scilicet, plenarias die primo ingressus, in mortis articulo, die festo principali a consororibus eligendo vel uno ex septem diebus subsequentibus, partiales septem annorum et totidem quadragenarum, quatuor anni diebus a consororibus similiter eligendis, sexaginta dierum quoties bonum aliquod opus iuxta institutum sodalitatis peregerint. Deinde S. V. eamdem Sodalitatem die 16 Ian. 1881, erexit ad dignitatem archisodalitatis cum iuribus consuetis, atque per duo rescripta 21 Iulii 1884 et 28 Martii 1886, addidit singulas indulgentias plenarias pro diebus festis Immaculatae Conceptionis B.V. — Epiphania D.N.J.C. — S. Josephi Sp. B.V. — S. Monicae — S. Annae B.V. Matris.

Quum autem permultae sodales, sive longiori intervallo, sive negotiis aliisve incommodis, saepius impediantur, quominus ecclesias adeant in ipsismet festis diebus; orator humillime petit, ut indulgentiae per rescripta dierum 20 Iulii 1884 et 28 Martii ut supra adnexae festis, a sodalibus acquiri possint vel ipso die festo, vel die dominica proxime sequenti aut festo de precepto inter octiduum festi occurrente.

Pro qua gratia.

Ex Audienta SSmi habita die 17 Februarii 1889.

SSmus Dominus Noster Leo, Divina Providentia PP. XIII, referente me infrascripto archiepiscopo Tyren., S. Congnis. de Propaganda Fide Secretario, benigne indulsit ut indulgentias iam obtentas lucrari valeant adscriptae die statuto vel etiam Dominica sequenti; in reliquis guadeant impetratis.

Datum Romae ex aedibus dictae S. Congnis. die et anno ut supra.

D. Archiep. Tyren. Secr.

Vidimus et promulgari permisimus.
Allegheniae die 4 Aprilis 1889.
†R. Phelan, V.G.
Coadj. Episc. Pittsb.
Gratis quocumque titulo

5. Rescript of March 13, 1892.

Beatissime Pater,

Hodiernus Moderator Prov. Min. Cap. Penn. in Statibus Americae Foederatis, ad pedes S. V. humiliter provolutus, quo Sodales Archiconfraternitatis Mat. Christ. in Ecclesia parochiali S. Augustini Min. Cap. Civitatis ac Dioc. Pittsburgensis, per rescriptum S. C. de Prop. Fide die Ian. 16 1881, rite erectae ac deinde Sacris Indulg. didatae magis ac magis in incoepta salutifera semita incitentur novas iterum a Benignitate Apostolica, summis precibus efflagitat gratias, videlicet: Indulgentiam plenariam (defunctis applicabilem) omnibus Sodalibus praefatae Archisodalitatis, quae rite expiratae ac sacra synaxi refectae, respectivam ecclesiam parochialem visitaverint ibique ad mentem S. V. pie oraverint, in festo B. M. V. Perdolentis, quae sub hoc vocabulo patrona est principalis praedictae Sodalitatis — item in festo S. Rosae Limanae Virg., eiusdem Sodalitatis patronae secundariae — necnon in festo Angelorum Custodum, qui pariter in secundarios Sodalitatis patronos selecti sunt.

Placeat insuper S. V., quod eas Indulgentias (prout pro aliis eidem Sodalitati elargitis benigne concessum est) diebus festivis ut supra adsignatis, aut etiam, in casu legitimi impedimenti, Dominica immediate insequenti lucrifacere possint ac valeant.

Qua de gratia.

Ex Audientia SSmi habita die 13 Martii 1892.

SSmus Dominus Noster Leo, Divina Providentia PP. XIII, referente me infrascripto S. Congnis. de Propaganda Fide Secretario, benigne adnuere dignatus est pro gratia in omnibus iuxta petita.

Datum Romae ex Aedibus dictae S. Congnis. die et anno ut supra.

Ignatius Archiep. Tamiathen.

Vidimus et promulgari permisimus.

Pittsburgii,

†R. Phelan

Episc. Pittsb.

Gratis quocumque titulo

6. Rescript of April 24, 1893.

Beatissime Pater,

Fr. Hyacinthus a Durachio Ord. Min. Cap. Prov. Penn. in America hodiernus Minister, S. V. post osculum Pedis humillime exponit quod ad Ecclesiam S. Augustini urbis et dioecesis Pitts. suae curae permissam, S. V. dignatus est erigere archisodalitatem Matrum Christianarum cum iure aggregandi cuius quidem Director consuevit diplomata aggregationum a se subscripta sigilloque munita tradere Secretario, transmittenda suo tempore Directoribus aggregationem petituris. Quum vero eo decreto S. Cong. Indulg. die 3 Decembris, 1892 iste modus ut validus non sit retinendus, humilis orator S. V. exorat, ut aggregationes hac vel illa de causa huiusque invalide peractas Apostolica benignitate sanare dignetur.

Et Deus....

Vigore specialium facultatum a SSmo D. N. Leone XIII tributorum, S. Cong. Indulg. sacrisque Reliquiis praeposita petitam sanationem benigne concessit. Contrariis quibuscumque non obstantibus.

Datum Romae ex secretaria eiusdem S. Cong. die 24 Aprilis, 1893.

L.S.

Aloisius Card. Sepiacci
Archiep. Nicopolit. Secretarius

7. Rescript of July 17, 1895.

Beatissime Pater, Hyacinthus a Durachio Minister Provinciae Capuccinorum Pennsilvania (America) ad pedes S. Tuae provolutus, pro sodalibus Archiconfraternitatis Matrum Christ. in Ecclesia Conventus Cap. in Pitt. rite erecta, humiliter implorat Indulgentiam plenariam die festo S. Joannis Baptistae (unius ex patronis secundariis dictae Sodalitates) ipso die festi vel Dominica subsequenti lucrandam sub consuetis conditionibus atque etiam animabus Purgationi applicandam.

Et Deus....

S. C. Indulgentiis Sacrisque Reliquiis praeposita, utendo facultatibus a SS. D. N. Leone PP. XIII sibi specialiter tributis, Plenariam Indulgentiam defunctis quoque applicabilem benigne convenit die festo S. Joannis Baptistae vel Dominica eumdem diem festum immediate sequenti lucrandam a sodalibus praedictae Archiconfraternitatis quae vere poenitentes, confessae ac S. Synaxi refectae aliquam Ecclesiam vel publicum Sacellum devote visitaverint et inibi pias ad Deum preces aliquamdiu effuderint ad mentem Sanctitatis Suae. Praesenti in perpetuum valituro absque ulla Brevis expeditione. Datum Romae ex Secretario euisdem S. C. die 17 Iulii 1895.

L.S.

Card. Bonaparte
A. Archiep. Nicopolit. Secret.

Vidimus et promulgari permisimus.
Pittsburgii, die XII mensis Augusti A. D. 1895.
†R. Phelan
Episc. Pittsb.

8. Papal Brief of January 27, 1905.

Pius PP. X.

Ad perpetuam rei memoriam. Quum, sicut accepimus ab hodierno Ministro Provinciae Minorum Ordinis S. Francisci Capulatorum Pennsylvaniae in America Septentrionali, in Ecclesia Deo sacra in honorem S. Augustini Episcopi Doctoris, civitatis et dioecesis Pittsburgensis, canonice erecta extet Archisodalitas Matrum Christianarum, quae iuxta sodalitii statuta certis quibusdam anni diebus Congregationem solent habere; Nos ut uberiori cum fructu animarum Congregationes huiusmodi peragantur, caelestes Ecclesiae thesauros, quorum dispensatores Nos esse voluit Altissimus, reserandos censuimus. Quare de Omnipotentis Dei misericordia ac BB. Petri et Pauli App. eius auctoritate confisi, omnibus et singulis mulieribus nunc et pro tempore eandem in Archisodalitatem adlectis, quo anni die congregationibus ex instituto societatis habendis, corde saltem contritae intererint, trecentos dies de iniunctis eis, seu alias quomodolibet debitis poenitentiis in forma Ecclesiae consueta relaxamus. Quas poenitentiarum relaxationes etiam animabus christifidelium quae Deo in charitate coniunctae ab hac luce migraverint, per modum suffragii applicari posse in Domino largimur. Contrariis non obstantibus quibuscumque. Praesentibus in perpetuum valituris. Datum Romae apud S. Petrum sub annulo Piscatoris die XXVII Ianuarii MDCCCCV.

Pontificatus Nostri anno secundo.

Pro Dno. Card. Macchi
Marini

9. Rescript of December 10, 1941.

(10601/'41)

Sacra Paenitentiaria Apostolica

Beatissime Pater,

Director Generalis archiconfraternitatis Matrum Christianarum, in ecclesia Sancti Augustini, intra fines dioecesis Pittsburgensis erectae, ad pedes Sanctitatis Tuae provolutus, humiliter petit Indulgentiam plenariam, a sodalibus, confessis ac sacra Synaxi refectis, die festo Maternitatis Beatae Mariae Virginis vel Dominica proxime subsequenti lucrandam, si aliquam ecclesiam vel publicum oratorium visitaverint et ad mentem Summi Pontificis preces fuderint.

Et Deus....

Die 10 Decembris 1941

Sacra Paenitentiaria Apostolica, vi facultatum a SSmo D. N. Pio PP. XII sibi tributarum, benigne annuit pro gratia iuxta preces in perpetuum, absque ulla Brevis expeditione. Contrariis quibuscumque non obstantibus.

De mandato Eminentissimi:
Luzio (Regens)
Rotti Secr.

Visum et approbatum
†Hugh C. Boyle
Episcopus Pittsburgensis

10. Rescript of June 21, 1955.

(3778/55)

Sacra Paenitentiaria Apostolica

Beatissime Pater,

Moderator Generalis Archisodalitatis Matrum Christianarum, in ecclesia Ordinis Fratrum Minorum Capuccinorum, urbis episcopalis Pittsburgensis, constitutae, ad pedes Sanctitatis tuae provolutus, humiliter petit *Indulgentiam plenariam,* a sodalibus memoratae consociationis suetis conditionibus lucrandam, diebus festis D. N. Jesu Christi Regis, S. Familiae, Annuntiationis et Septem Dolorum Beatae Mariae Virginis (feria VI[a] post dominicam Passionis), B.M.V. Reginae, S. Elisabeth et S. Gerardi Majella. Petit insuper, in favorem sodalium infra relatas invocationes recitantium, *Indulgentiam trecentorum dierum,* saltem corde contrito lucrandam, necnon *Indulgentiam plenariam,* ab iisdem semel in mense conditionibus consuetis acquirendam, si easdem preces quotidie recitaverint:

"O Maria, Immaculata Virgo et Mater Dolorosa, commenda perdilectos liberos nostros Sacratissimo Cordi Iesu, qui Matri Suae nihil denegat. Ora pro eis.

"Sancti Custodes, Orate pro eis.

"Sancte Ioseph, Patrone potentissime, Ora pro eis.

"S. Ioannes, perdilecte discipule Cordis Iesu, Ora pro eis.

"S. Augustine, o.p.eis—S. Antoni, o.p.eis—Sancte Aloysi, o.p.eis—S. Anna, Mater Mariae, o.p.eis—S. Elisabeth, o.p.eis—S. Monica, ora pro eis."

Et Deus....

Die 21 Iunii 1955

Sacra Paenitentiaria Apostolica, vi facultatum a SS. D. N. Pio PP. XII sibi tributarum benigne annuit pro gratia iuxta preces. Contrariis quibuslibet non obstantibus.

de mandato Eminentissimi:
Luzio (Regens)
Rotti, Secr.

Procura Capp. Prot. No. 298/55

BIBLIOGRAPHY

Sources

Acta Apostolicae Sedis, Commentarium Officiale, Romae, 1909—

Acta Sanctae Sedis, 41 vols., Romae, 1865-1908.

Analecta Iuris Pontificii, Romae, Parisiis, 1855-1890.

Analecta Ordinis Fratrum Minorum Capuccinorum, Romae, 1885—

Bullarii Franciscani Epitome seu Summa Bullarum et Supplementum, ed. Conrad Eubel, Quaracchi, 1908.

Bullarium Carmelitanum plures complectens Summorum Pontificum Constitutiones ad Ordinem Fratrum Beatissimae Dei Genitricis de Monte Carmelo Spectantes, 2 vols., Romae, 1715-1768.

Bullarium Franciscanum, vols. I-IV, ed. Joanne Sbaraglia, Romae, 1759-1768; vols. V-VII, ed. Conrad Eubel, Romae, 1898-1904; Series Nova, vol. I, ed. Ulricus Huentemann, Quaracchi, 1929; vols. II-III, ed. Joseph M. Pou y Marti, Quaracchi, 1939-1949.

Bullarium Ordinis Eremitarum S. Augustini, Romae, 1628.

Bullarium Ordinis FF. Minorum S. P. Francisci Capuccinorum, vols. I-VII, Romae, 1740-1752; vols. VIII-X, Oeniponte, 1883-1884.

Bullarium Ordinis FF. Praedicatorum, ed. Thomas Ripoll et Antonius Bremond, 8 vols., Romae, 1729-1740.

Bullarum Diplomatum et Privilegiorum Romanorum Pontificum Taurinensis Editio, 25 vols., Augustae Taurinorum, 1857-1872.

Canones et Decreta Sacrosancti Oecumenici Concilii Tridentini, Romae, 1882.

Codex Iuris Canonici Pii X Pontificis Maximi Iussu Digestus Benedicti Papae XV Auctoritate Promulgatus, Romae: Typis Polyglottis Vaticanis, 1917.

Codex Theodosianus cum perpetuis commentariis Iacobi Gothofredi, editio nova in VI tomos digesta, Lipsiae, 1743.

Codicis Iuris Canonici Fontes cura Emi Petri Card. Gasparri editi, 9 vols., Romae, (postea Civitate Vaticana): Typis Polyglottis Vaticanis, 1923-1939. (Vols. VII-IX, ed. *cura et studio Emi Iustiniani Card. Serédi.*)

Corpus Christianorum Series Latina, Turnholti: Typographi Brepols, Editores Pontificii, 1954—

Corpus Iuris Canonici, editio Lipsiensis secunda, post Aemilii Ludovici Richteri curas instruxit Aemilius Friedberg, 2 vols., Lipsiae: ex Officina Bernhardi Tauchnitz, 1879-1881; ed. anastatice repetita, 1928.

Corpus Iuris Civilis, 3 vols., Berolini: apud Weidmannos, 1928-1929. Vol. I, *Institutiones,* ed. stereotypa 15. recognovit P. Krueger; *Digesta,* ed. stereotypa 15. recognovit Theodorus Mommsen; Vol. II, *Codex Justinianus,* ed. stereotypa 10. recognovit et retractavit P. Krueger; Vol. III, *Novellae Constitutiones,* ed. stereotypa 5. R. Schoell; opus Schoellii morte interceptum absolvit G. Kroll.

Decreta Authentica Congregationis Sacrorum Rituum, 6 vols., Romae, 1898-1927.

Decreta Authentica Sacrae Congregationis Indulgentiis Sacrisque Reliquiis ab Anno

1668 *ad Annum* 1882, edita jussu et auctoritate Sanctissimi D. N. Leonis P.P. XIII, Ratisbonae, Neo Eboraci, Cincinnatii: Pustet, 1883.

Denziger, H., et Bannwart, C., et Umberg, J., *Enchiridion Symbolorum, Definitionum, et Declarationum de Rebus Fidei et Morum*, 24-25. ed., Friburgi-Brisgoviae: Herder, 1948.

Documenta Apostolica Archisodalitatis Matrum Christianarum, Pittsburgii ad Sancti Augustini Ecclesiam, 1886.

Leonis XIII Pontificis Maximi Acta, 22 vols., Romae: Typographia Vaticana, 1881-1903.

Litterae Apostolicae Motu Proprio Datae ad Venerabiles Fratres Patriarchas, Archiepiscopos, Episcopos, Ceterosque Locorum Hierarchas Ecclesiarum Orientalium, Pacem et Communionem Cum Apostolica Sede Habentes: de Ritibus Orientalibus, de Personis, pro Ecclesiis Orientalibus, Adnotationibus Fontium Auctae cura Pontificii Consilii Codici Iuris Canonici Orientalis Redigendo, Romae: Typis Polyglottis Vaticanis, 1957.

Magnum Bullarium Romanum, seu eiusdem Continuatio, 19 vols., Luxemburg, 1727-1758.

Mansi, Joannes, *Sacrorum Conciliorum Nova et Amplissima Collectio*, 53 vols. in 59, Parisiis-Arnhem-Leipzig, 1901-1927.

Manual for Directors and Officers, Confraternity of Christian Mothers, Pittsburgh: The Archconfraternity of Christian Mothers, 1957.

Manual for the Establishment and Direction of Confraternities of Christian Mothers, Pittsburgh: The Archconfraternity of Christian Mothers, 1911.

Migne, J. P., *Patrologiae Cursus Completus, Series Graeca*, 161 vols., Parisiis, 1856-1866.

........................, *Patrologiae Cursus Completus, Series Latina*, 221 vols., Parisiis, 1844-1864.

Monumenta Germaniae Historica, Hannoverae-Lipsiae-Berolini, 1826—

—*Epistolae Selectae, I, S. Bonifatii et Lulli Epistolae*, ed. Michael Tangl, Berolini, 1916.

—*Leges*, 5 vols., 1835-1889; Vol. I, *Capitularia Regum Francorum*, ed. Georgius Henricus Pertz, Hannoverae, 1863, Neudruck, 1925; Vol. III, *Leges Nationum Germanicarum*, ed. J. Merkel, 1863, Neudruck, 1925.

—*Leges: Legum Sectio I, Leges Nationum Germanicarum*, Tom. I, *Leges Visigothorum*, ed. K. Zeumer, 1902; *Legum Sectio III, Concilia*, Tom. II, recensivit Albertus Werminghoff, 1893.

Prinzivalli, A., *Resolutiones seu Decreta Authentica S. Congregationis Indulgentiis Sacrisque Reliquiis Praepositae ab anno* 1668 *ad annum* 1861 *accurate collecta*, Romae, 1862.

Schneider, Josephus, *Rescripta Authentica Sacrae Congregationis Indulgentiis Sacrisque Reliquiis Praepositae*, Ratisbonae, Neo Eboraci et Cincinnatii: Pustet, 1885.

Authors

Abbo, J.-Hannan, J., *The Sacred Canons: A Concise Presentation of the Current Disciplinary Norms of the Church*, 2 vols., rev. ed., St. Louis: B. Herder Book Co., 1957.

Adone, A., *Synopsis Canonico-Liturgica,* Neapoli, 1866.

Augustine, Charles, *A Commentary on the New Code of Canon Law,* 8 vols., St. Louis: B. Herder Book Co., 1925-1938.

Barbosa, A., *Iuris Ecclesiastici Universi Libri III,* Lugduni, 1660.

......................., *Variae Tractationes Iuris,* 5 vols. in 1, Lugduni, 1631.

Bassi, John Baptist, *Tractatus de Sodalitiis,* Romae, 1725.

Beil, Josef, *Das Kirchliche Vereinsrecht,* Paderborn: Schoeningh, 1932.

Beringer, Franz, *Die Ablaesse, Ihr Wesen und Gebrauch,* bearbeitet von P. Steinen, 2 vols., Paderborn: Schoeningh, 1921-1922.

Beste, Udalricus, *Introductio in Codicem,* 2. ed., Collegeville, Minn.: St. John's Abbey Press, 1944.

Blat, Alberto, *Commentarium Textus Codicis Iuris Canonici,* 6 vols., Romae: Collegio "Angelico," 1921-1927.

Borkowski, Aurelius L., *De Confraternitatibus Ecclesiasticis,* Washingtonii: Universitas Catholica Americae, 1918.

Bouscaren, T. L.-Ellis, A., *Canon Law, A Text and Commentary,* 3. ed., Milwaukee: Bruce Publishing Co., 1957.

—*Canon Law Digest,* Vols. I-III; Bouscaren and James O'Connor, Vol. IV and supplements; Milwaukee: Bruce Publishing Co., 1934-1960.

Bouvier, *Traité Dogmatique et Pratique des indulgences, des confréries et du jubilé,* Paris, 1855.

Campelo, P. J., *De Indulgentiis Seraphici Ordinis,* 3. ed., Compostellae: Typis "El Eco Franciscano," 1958.

Cappello, Felix, *Summa Iuris Canonici in Usum Scholarum Concinnata,* 3 vols., 4. ed., Romae: apud Aedes Universitatis Gregorianae, 1945-1955.

Chelodi, Joannes-Ciprotti, Pius, *Ius Canonicum de Personis,* 5. ed., Vicenza: Società Anonima Tipografica, 1947.

Cicognani, Amleto, *Canon Law,* 2. ed., Revised, English Version by J. O'Hara and F. Brennan, Westminster, Maryland: Newman Press, 1949, Reprint of 2. ed., Philadelphia: Dolphin Press, 1935.

Claeys Boúúaert, F.-Simenon, G., *Manuale Iuris Canonici,* 3 vols., Gandae et Leodii: apud Auctores, 1939-1947.

Clarke, Thomas J., *Parish Societies,* The Catholic University of America Canon Law Studies, n. 176, Washington, D.C.: The Catholic University of America Press, 1943.

Cocchi, G., *Commentarium in Codicem Iuris Canonici ad Usum Scholarum,* 4. ed., 8 vols., Taurinorum Augustae: Marietti, 1931-1946.

Coli, Ugo, *Collegia e Sodalitates,* Bologna: Presso Il Seminario Giuridico, 1913.

De Meester, A., *Iuris Canonici et Iuris Canonico-Civilis Compendium,* 3 vols. in 4, Brugis: Desclée, 1921-1928.

Dictionnaire D'Archéologie Chrétienne et De Liturgie, 15 toms. in 30, Paris: Letouzey et Ané, 1924-1953.

Dictionnaire de Droit Canonique, Paris: Letouzey et Ané, 1935—

Dictionnaire Pratique Connaissances Religieuses, 6 toms., Paris: Letouzey et Ané, 1925-1928.

Duchesne, L., *The Early History of the Church,* 3. ed., 3 vols., London: John Murray Co., 1931.

Ebner, Adalbert, *Die Kloesterlichen Gebetsverbruederungen,* Regensburg, 1890.

Eichmann, E.-Moersdorf, K., *Lehrbuch des Kirchenrecht,* 7. ed., 3 vols., Paderborn: Schoeningh, 1953-1954.

Fanfani, L., *De Confraternitatibus Aliisque Associationibus Ordinis FF. Praedicatorum Propriis,* Romae, 1934.

......................., *De Iure Religiosorum,* Rovigo: Istituto Padano di Arti Grafiche, 1949.

Ferraris, L., *Prompta Bibliotheca, Canonica, Iuridica, Moralis, Theologica necnon Ascetica, Polemica, Rubricistica, Historica,* 9 vols., Romae, 1885-1899.

Ferreres, J. B., *Las Cofradías y Congregaciones Eclesiasticas Según la Disciplina Vigente,* Barcelona: Gustavo Gili, 1907.

Fournier, P.-Le Bras, G., *Histoire des Collections Canoniques en Occident,* 2 vols., Paris: Recueil Sirey, 1931-1932.

Gelcich, *Le Confraternite Laiche in Dalmazia et Specialmente Quelli di Marinai,* Ragusa, 1885.

Gougnard, A., *Tractatus de Indulgentiis,* 5. ed., Mechliniae: H. Dessain, 1933.

Goyeneche, S., *Quaestiones Canonicae de Iure Religiosorum,* 2 vols., Neapoli: M. D'Auria Pontificius Editor, 1954-1955.

Hefele, Charles-Leclercq, Henri, *Histoire des Conciles,* 11 vols in 20, Paris: Librairie Letouzey et Ané, 1907-1949.

Jone, H., *Commentarium in Codicem Iuris Canonici,* 3 vols., Paderborn: Officina Libraria F. Schoeningh, 1950-1955.

Kurtscheid, B., *Historia Iuris Canonici, Historia Institutorum,* 2. ed., Romae: Catholic Book Agency, 1951.

Lambert, J., *Two Thousand Years of Gild Life,* London: Hull, 1891.

Lexicon fuer Theologie und Kirche, 10 vols., Freiburg im Breisgau: Herder & Co., 1930-1938.

Maroto, P., *Institutiones Iuris Canonici ad Normam Novi Codicis,* 2 vols., Romae: apud Commentarium pro Religiosis, 1921.

Matthaeus Conte a Coronata, *Institutiones Iuris Canonici,* 5 vols., Vol. I, 4. ed., Taurini: Marietti, 1950.

Matulenas, R., *Communication—A Source of Privileges,* The Catholic University of America Canon Law Studies, n. 183, Washington, D.C.: The Catholic University of America Press, 1943.

Michiels, Gommarus, *Normae Generales Iuris Canonici,* 2. ed., 2 vols., Parisiis-Tornaci-Romae: Desclée et Socii, 1949.

......................., *Principia Generalia de Personis in Ecclesia,* 2. ed., Parisiis-Tornaci-Romae: Desclée et Socii, 1955.

Mocchegiani, P., *Collectio Indulgentiarum Theologice, Canonice et Historice Digesta,* 3. ed., Ad Claras Aquas, 1897.

Monti, G., *Le Confraternite Medievali dell'Alta e Media Italia,* 2 vols., Firenze: "La Nuova Italia" Editrice, 1927.

Muratori, L., *Antiquitates Italicae Medii Aevi,* 6 vols., Mediolani, 1738-1743.

Ojetti, B., *Commentarium in Codicem Iuris Canonici,* 4 vols., Romae, 1927-1931.

Phillips, G., *Kirchenrecht,* 7 vols., Regensburg, 1845-1872.

Pignatelli, J., *Consultationes Canonicae*, 11 vols. in 4, Coloniae Allobrogum, 1700.

Pruemmer, D., *Manuale Iuris Canonici*, 4. ed., Friburgi Brisgoviae: B. Herder & Co., 1927.

Quigley, J., *Condemned Societies*, The Catholic University of America Canon Law Studies, n. 46, Washington, D.C.: The Catholic University of America Press, 1927.

Reiffenstuel, A., *Ius Canonicum Universum*, 5 vols. in 7, Parisiis, 1864-1870.

Reinmann, G., *The Third Order Secular of St. Francis*, The Catholic University of America Canon Law Studies, n. 50, Washington, D.C.: The Catholic University of America, 1928.

Regatillo, E., *Institutiones Iuris Canonici*, 5. ed., 2 vols., Santander: Editorial Sal Terrae, 1956.

........................, *Interpretatio et Iurisprudentia Codicis Iuris Canonici*, 3. ed., Santander: "Sal Terrae," 1953.

Ritterus, P., *De Confraternitate*, Jenae, 1614.

Rodericus, E., *Quaestiones Regulares et Canonicae*, 2 vols., Venetiis, 1611.

Rush, A., *Death and Burial in Christian Antiquity*, The Catholic University of America Studies in Christian Antiquity, n. 1, Washington, D.C.: The Catholic University of America Press, 1941.

Sagmueller, J., *Lehrbuch des Katholischen Kirchenrechts*, 4. ed., 2 vols., Freiburg im Breisgau, 1925-1934.

Scaduto, F., *Confraternite*, Torino, 1886.

Schaefer, T., *De Religiosis ad Normam Codicis Iuris Canonici*, 4. ed., Romae: Typis Polyglottis Vaticanis, 1947.

Schmalzgrueber, F., *Ius Ecclesiasticum Universum*, 5 vols. in 12, Romae, 1843-1845.

Schnuerer, G., *Kirche und Kultur in Mittelalter*, 3 vols., Paderborn: Schoeningh, 1927-1929.

Schreiber, Paul F., *Canonical Precedence*, The Catholic University of America Canon Law Studies, n. 408, Washington, D.C.: The Catholic University of America Press, 1961.

Seeberger, M., *Key to the Spiritual Treasures*, 2. ed., Collegeville, Ind.: St. Joseph's College Printing Office, 1897.

Seraphinus de Angelis, *De Fidelium Associationibus*, 2 vols., Neapoli: M. D"Auria Pontificius Editor, 1959.

........................, *De Indulgentiis*, editio altera, Città del Vaticano: Libreria Editrice Vaticana, 1950.

Sipos, S., *Enchiridion Iuris Canonici*, 6. ed. recognovit Ladislaus Galos, Romae: Orbis Catholicus-Herder, 1954.

Smith, T., *English Gilds*, London, 1870.

Tachy, A., *Traité des Confréries*, Amiens: Jourdain-Rousseau, 1896.

Tamassi, *L'Affratellamento*, Torino, 1886.

Toso, A., *Ad Codicem Iuris Canonici ... Commentaria Minora*, 5 vols. in 2, Taurini-Romae: Marietti, 1920-1934.

Van Espen, Z., *Compendium Iuris Ecclesiastici*, 2 vols., Bassani, 1784.

Van Hove, A., *Commentarium Lovaniense in Codicem Iuris Canonici*, I vol. in 5 toms., Mechliniae-Romae: H. Dessain, 1928-1939; Tom. V, *De Privilegiis, De Dispensationibus,* 1939.

Vasto, B., *De Communicatione Privilegiorum,* Dissertatio historico-canonica ad lauream in facultate Iuris Canonici Pontificiae Universitate Gregorianae, n. 161, Aquilae in Vestinis, 1936.

Vermeersch, A.-Creusen, I., *Epitome Iuris Canonici,* 7. ed., 3 vols., Mechliniae-Romae: H. Dessain, 1949-1956.

Vromant, G.-Bongaerts, L., *De Fidelium Associationibus,* 2. ed., Parisiis: Desclée de Brouwer, 1955.

Wernz, F. X., *Ius Decretalium ad Usum Praelectionum in Scholis Textus Iuris Canonici sive Iuris Decretalium,* 6 vols., Romae, 1905-1914, Vol. III, 2. ed., 1908.

Wernz, F. X.-Vidal, P., *Ius Canonicum,* 7 vols. in 8, Romae: Universitas Gregoriana, 1933-1952; Vol. III, *De Religiosis,* 1933.

Westlake, H. F., *The Parish Guilds of Medieval England,* London, 1929.

Zumbo, G., *Delle Confraternite Ecclesiastiche,* Roma, 1909.

Articles

Anonymous, "Commentarium," *NRTh,* XXV (1893), pp. 140-159.

Amanieu, A., "Archiconfrérie," *DDC,* I (1935), cols. 934-948.

Boudinhon, A., "Des Confréries, III, de l'agrégation ou affiliation des confréries," *Le Canoniste Contemporain,* XIII (1890), pp. 302-309.

Bricout, J., "Mères Chrétiennes (Archiconfrérie)," *DPCR,* IV (1926), cols. 898-900.

Creusen, J., "Associations Pieuses," *DDC,* I (1935), cols. 1270-1285.

Duhr, J., "La Confrérie dans la vie d'Église," *RHE,* XXXV[1] (1939), pp. 435-478.

Durand, H., "Confrérie," *DDC,* IV (1944), cols. 128-176.

Klens, H., "Muettervereine," *Lexicon fuer Theologie und Kirche,* VII (1935), 399.

Lambert, A., "Apotactites et Apotaxaménes," *DACL,* I[2] (1924), cols. 2604-2626.

Larraona, A., "Commentarium Codicis, canon 491," *CpR,* IV (1923), 210-218; 273-280.

Le Bras, G., "Les Confréries Chrétiennes: Problèmes et Propositions," *RHDFE,* XIX (1940-1941), pp. 310-363.

Leclercq, H., "Confréries," *DACL,* III[2] (1948), cols. 2553-2560.

........................, "Fossoyeurs," *DACL,* V[2] (1923), cols. 2065-2092.

........................, "Parabalani," *DACL,* XIII[2] (1938), cols. 1574-1578.

Mallet, S., "Some Ancient Benedictine Confraternity Books," *Downside Review,* IV (1885), pp. 2-14.

Meersseman, G., "Etudes sur les anciennes confréries Dominicaines: I. Les Confréries de Saint Dominique," *Archivum Fratrum Praedicatorum,* XX (1950), pp. 5-113.

........................, "Études sur les anciennes confréries Dominicaines: II. Les Confréries de Saint-Pierre Martyr," *Archivum Fratrum Praedicatorum,* XXI (1951), pp. 51-196.

........................, "La Prédication Dominicaine dans les Congrégations Mariales en Italie au XIIIe siècle," *Archivum Fratrum Praedicatorum,* XVIII (1948), pp. 130-161.

Vermeersch, A., "Annotationes," *Periodica,* XVI (1927), pp. 56-59.

Periodicals

Archivum Fratrum Praedicatorum, Romae, 1931—

Commentarium pro Religiosis, Romae, 1920-1934; *Commentarium pro Religiosis et Missionariis*, Romae, 1935—

Downside Review, Downside Abbey, Bath, 1880—

Il Monitore Ecclesiastico, Romae, 1876-1948; *Monitor Ecclesiasticus*, Romae, 1949—

La Cononiste Contemporain, Paris, 1878-1926.

Nouvelle Revue Théologique, Paris, 1869—

Periodica de Religiosis et Missionariis, Brugis, 1905-1919; *Periodica de Re Canonica et Morali, utilia praesertim Religiosis et Missionariis*, Brugis, 1920-1927; *Periodica de Re Morali, Canonica, Liturgica*, Brugis, 1927-1936; Romae, 1937—

Revue d'Historie ecclésiastique, Louvain, 1900—

Revue Historique de Droit Français et Étranger, Paris, 1855—

Tertius Ordo, Romae, 1940—

ABBREVIATIONS

AAS—Acta Apostolicae Sedis.

ASS—Acta Sanctae Sedis.

BOE S. Aug.—Bullarium Ordinis Eremitarum S. Augustini.

Bull. Carm.—Bullarium Carmelitanum.

Bull. Fran.—Bullarium Franciscanum.

Bull. Fran. Epit.—Bullarii Franciscani Epitome.

Bull. Praed.—Bullarium Ordinis FF. Praedicatorum.

Bull. Rom. Taur.—Bullarum Diplomatum et Privilegiorum Romanorum Sanctorum Pontificum Taurinensis Editio.

C—Codex Justinianus.

CLD—Canon Law Digest.

CpR—Commentarium pro Religiosis.

C. Th.—Codex Theodosianus.

D—Digesta Justiniana.

DACL—Dictionnaire D'Archéologie Chrétienne et De Liturgie.

DDC—Dictionnaire de Droit Canonique.

DPCR—Dictionnaire Pratique Connaissances Religieuses.

Fontes—Codicis Iuris Canonici Fontes, Gasparri-Serédi.

Mansi—*Sacrorum Conciliorum Nova et Amplissima Collectio.*

MGH—Monumenta Germaniae Historica.

MPG—Migne, *Patrologiae Cursus Completus, Series Graeca.*

MPL—Migne, *Patrologiae Cursus Completus, Series Latina.*

N—Novellae Justinianae.

NRTh—Nouvelle Revue Théologique.

PCI—Pontifical Commission for the Authentic Interpretation of the Code of Canon Law.

RHDFE—Revue Historique de Droit Français et Étranger.

RHE—Revue d'Historie ecclésiastique.
S. C. C.—Sacra Congregatio Concilii.
S. C. Ep. et Reg.—Sacra Congregatio Episcoporum et Regularium.
S. C. Indulg.—Sacra Congregatio Indulgentiarum.
S. C. P. F.—Sacra Congregatio de Propaganda Fide.
S. R. C.—Sacrorum Rituum Congregatio.
S. R. R.—Sacra Romana Rota.

ALPHABETICAL INDEX

INDEX OF CANONS

BIOGRAPHICAL NOTE

Edmund William Quinn was born in Beaver Falls, Pennsylvania, August 17, 1926. He attended Saint Mary's Elementary School in that city and graduated in 1940. He then entered Saint Fidelis College and Seminary, the seminary of the Capuchin Fathers in Herman, Pennsylvania. After graduating in 1946 he entered the Capuchin Novitiate in Cumberland, Maryland, pronouncing his vows on July 14, 1947. Philosophical studies were pursued at Saint Fidelis Seminary, Victoria, Kansas, and at Saint Fidelis College, Herman, Pennsylvania. Upon completion of his course of theology at Capuchin College, Washington, D.C., he was ordained to the priesthood in Saint Gabriel's Church, Washington, D.C., June 24, 1952. After teaching two years at Saint Francis Minor Seminary, Victoria, Kansas, he entered the Gregorian University, Rome, Italy, receiving the degree of Bachelor of Canon Law in June of 1956, and the degree of Licentiate in Canon Law in June of 1957. After teaching a year in Saint Francis Minor Seminary, Victoria, Kansas, he enrolled in the School of Canon Law at The Catholic University of America in September of 1958.

CANON LAW STUDIES*

421. Quinn, Rev. Edmund, O.F.M. Cap., B.A., J.C.L.
Archconfraternities, archsodalities and primary unions, with a supplement on the Archconfraternity of Christian Mothers.
422. Brady, Rev. Mel Lawrence, O.F.M., B.A., J.C.L.,
The quinquennial report of religious institutes to the Holy See.
423. Brenkle, Rev. John J., B.A., J.C.L.,
The impediment of male impotence, with special application to paraplegia.
424. Christensen, Rev. Joseph Edward, J.C.L.,
Character requisites for reception of holy orders. (microfilm)
425. Paul, Rev. John J., M.S.C., S.T.L., J.C.L.,
The recipient of the sacrament of penance. (microfilm)
426. Pavloff, Rev. George G., A.B., J.C.L.,
Papal judge delegates at the time of the *Corpus Iuris Canonici.*
427. Reissner, Rev. Edward A., A.B., J.C.L.,
Canonical employer-employee relationship: Canon 1524.
428. Schierse, Rev. Paul J., A.B., J.C.L.,
Laws of the State of Delaware affecting church property.
429. Seasoltz, Rev. Robert Kevin, O.S.B., A.B., S.T.L., J.C.L.,
Directives on sacred art and the building of a church. (microfilm)

*For a complete list of the available numbers of this series apply to The Catholic University of America Press, 620 Michigan Avenue, N.E., Washington 17, D.C., for a general catalogue.

www.ingramcontent.com/pod-product-compliance
Lightning Source LLC
LaVergne TN
LVHW050218080826
844660LV00012B/431

9780813225784